# The Cultural World of the Prophets

# The Cultural World
# of the Prophets

## The First Reading
## and the Responsorial Psalm

Sunday by Sunday,
*Year A*

John J. Pilch

LITURGICAL PRESS
Collegeville, Minnesota

www.litpress.org

Year A: ISBN 0-8146-2786-2
Year B: ISBN 0-8146-2787-0
Year C: ISBN 0-8146-2788-9

1    2    3    4    5    6    7    8

**Library of Congress Cataloging-in-Publication Data**

Pilch, John J.
    The cultural world of the prophets: the first reading and the responsorial psalm / John J. Pilch.
      p. cm.
    Includes bibliographical references.
    Contents: Sunday by Sunday, Year B.
    ISBN 0-8146-2787-0 (alk. paper)
    1. Bible. O.T.–Criticism, interpretation, etc. 2. Bible. O.T.–History of biblical events. 3. Middle East–Civilization–To 622. 4. Catholic Church. Lectionary for Mass (U.S.). Year C. I. Title.

BS1171.3.P55 2002
264'.34–dc21

                2002028667

*For*

*Marilou Seña-Ibita*
*and*
*Maricel Seña-Ibita*
*Manila, Philippines*

*Beloved* apó *who share* abuelo's *passion*
*for improving preaching*

# Contents

# Introduction

When I wrote *The Cultural World of Jesus, Sunday by Sunday,* 3 volumes (The Liturgical Press, 1995–97), I resolved to write a companion series: *The Cultural World of the Apostles, The Second Reading, Sunday by Sunday,* 3 volumes (The Liturgical Press, 2001–03). My intention was to provide the average person with a handy study guide first for the gospel readings, then later for the second readings in the liturgy every Sunday which are drawn chiefly from letters. Since it was becoming and still is increasingly difficult for adults to find free time during the week to attend a study group or lecture series on the Bible, I thought that a six-hundred word essay on the Scripture heard at liturgy on Sunday could be manageable and interesting. A person could read that while sitting in the pew before the liturgy began. If the homily wasn't working out well, a person could read the reflection in its place.

That the booklets have been useful for preachers, catechists, liturgists, and others as well came as a pleasant and welcome surprise. My publisher's suggestion to write a series on the first readings in the liturgy Sunday by Sunday, *The Cultural World of the Prophets,* also came as a surprise. The gospels and the second readings in Sunday liturgies present selections in a continuous or semicontinuous sequence that facilitates an orderly study of a gospel or a letter of an apostle, Sunday by Sunday.

In contrast, the selection and arrangement of the first readings in Sunday liturgies do not lend themselves to a similar study program. Yet the Old Testament passages are of significance in Christian worship. With this volume I turn to the task of offering insight into these Old Testament passages, a task of interest to me since graduate school. At the beginning of the second year in my first teaching position after completing my degree with a specialty in the New Testament (the letters of Paul), the dean asked if I could teach Old Testament courses. If not, my year-to-year contract would not be renewed, since he had just hired a Harvard graduate to teach New Testament and now needed someone to teach Old Testament. Well, of course I could teach the Old Testament! My graduate training at Marquette University was quite broad compared to other institutions. My Old Testament teachers included J. Coert Rylersdaam, Roland Murphy, O.CARM., Robert North, S.J., Thomas Caldwell, S.J., John F. X. Sheehan, S.J., and Gordon Bahr, among others. An article I published in *Harvard Theological Review* as a graduate student critically reviewed a scholarly study of Martin Luther's *Commentaries on the Psalms*. In all the years that have passed since beginning the serious study of Scripture, I have maintained a balanced interest in the entire Bible.

As a rule, the first reading—mainly though not always from the Old Testament—has been chosen in order to harmonize, in a more or less explicit way, with the doctrine and events recounted in the gospel. At times the connection is very slim, and in addition to that, the selections are drawn from all over the Old Testament. The readings are neither continuous nor semicontinuous. Biblical scholars and liturgists have lamented that the Old Testament does not get a fair hearing in the liturgy. From a modern, historically oriented point of view, this is correct. The gospel controls the selection of the first reading in Sunday liturgies. There is no escaping the impression that the gospel is considered more important in our worship service. That conviction, however, has some ancient roots. Theodore Abu Qurrah, Bishop of Haran (d. ninth century C.E.), the town from where Abraham departed for Canaan, wrote:

> Were it not for the Gospel, we would not have acknowledged Moses to be from God. Rather, on reflection, we would have vigorously opposed him. Likewise, we have

acknowledged the prophets to be from God because of the Gospel. It is not on the basis of reason, since we have acknowledged them because Christ has informed us that they are prophets. Also, because we have knowledge of Christ's whole economy, and having read their books and discovered that they had previously described his whole economy just as he accomplished it, we have acknowledged that they are prophets. At this point in time we do not acknowledge Christ and his affairs because of the books of the prophets. Rather, we acknowledge them because of Christ's saying that they are prophets and because of our own recognition that his economy is written in their books.[1]

Just as in the volumes of my other *The Cultural World of . . .* series, so too here, I present the reader with a thumbnail sketch of the literary context and historical setting of each Scripture text segment as it contributes to understanding the selected verses. I also present cultural information, at length when necessary (for example, see the discussion of Psalm 138 on the Twenty-First Sunday in Ordinary Time; for more details see John J. Pilch, "A Window into the Biblical World: No Thank You!" *The Bible Today* 40:1 [2002] 49–53), which is indispensable for understanding those verses appropriately and which is usually unavailable in other commentaries or resources. That kind of cultural information is what has made this series distinctive. I include similar brief reflections on the responsorial psalm, and for each Sunday I indicate the apparent link ("more or less explicit") by which the gospel should be associated with the first reading. There may indeed be links or associations other than those I have indicated. Finally, the Sundays marked with an asterisk (*) were assigned readings that are repeated in each Year of the Lectionary Cycle. I will repeat these reflections substantially unchanged in the other volumes of this series just as I did in the

[1] Quoted from Bruce J. Malina, "Three Theses for a More Adequate Reading of the New Testament," *Practical Theology: Perspectives from the Plains,* ed. Michael G. Lawler and Gail S. Risch (Omaha: Creighton University Press, 2000) 33–60.

volumes of the previous series (*The Cultural World of Jesus* and *The Cultural World of the Apostles*).

I am grateful to the Liturgical Press for publishing and promoting my cultural reflections and to the readers around the world who continue to welcome and to benefit from these publications. I believe that together, we all have taken some important steps toward realizing a goal that I set for myself upon completing my graduate studies: to contribute toward improving preaching.

Feast of St. Bernardine                                 John J. Pilch
  of Sienna, O.F.M.                          Georgetown University
May 20, 2003             The University of Pretoria, South Africa
                              and Studium Biblicum Franciscanum,
                                          Hong Kong, SAR, China

# First Sunday of Advent
## Isaiah 2:1-5

The Old Testament readings in Advent are presented in the Lectionary and interpreted in Christian tradition as prophecies about the Messiah and the messianic age. It is well to recall that prophets were chiefly spokespersons for the will of God in their contemporary time and place. The prophet spoke God's intentions for his "here and now." Like all peasants, so too Mediterranean peasants had no concept of a distant future. The pressing needs of living at a subsistence level constrained them to imagine only what is forthcoming from a present event such a birth from a pregnancy or harvest from a crop already planted. Thus Isaiah's announcement of imminent doom such as invasion and devastation by Assyria was realized in his lifetime and that of his original listeners (Isaiah 1). So too the phrase "in days to come" (Isa 2:2) points not to an event in the long distant future, but rather to something forthcoming soon.

The hope (which antedated Isaiah) is that Zion-Jerusalem will finally become the source of peace for the whole world. The time of Jesus' birth was a time of relative peace in the ancient world. Mediterranean believers always find answers to present events in the past. Reading Isaiah in the first century C.E. convinced believers that they were living in the time Isaiah described. Thus, from Zion-Jerusalem the LORD will judge everyone fairly because God's instruction (Torah) instructs all in the proper way to behave so as to insure peace. Difficulties will be resolved not by war, violence, or oppression

1

but by God's wise judgments. All the nations will learn peace from Jerusalem and will live it effectively. As today's gospel points out (Matt 24:37-44), since only God knows when future events such as a final judgment will take place, it is best for human beings to always be prepared. Such a state of preparation which would certainly include being rid of divisive ideologies and behaviors is without doubt an effective step in the right direction.

### Responsorial Psalm 122:1-2, 3-4, 4-5, 6-7, 8-9

Today's verses are drawn from the last of the Zion Psalms (26; 48; 76; 84; 86; 122). They praise the holy city, Jerusalem (vv. 3-5). The concluding verses (6-9) pray for the peace of Jerusalem in a Hebrew phrase that pairs sounds and words in a way that works a calming yet yearning effect in the mouth of the speaker and the ear of the listener: "sha'alu shalom yerushalaim." This psalm is a fitting bridge between Isaiah's aspirations for the Holy City and Jesus' warnings about that same Holy City's destruction in today's gospel. It would seem that this hope still remains elusive for Jerusalem.

# Second Sunday of Advent
## *Isaiah 11:1-10*

Once again the prophet describes the ideal king who will eventually appear and contrast starkly with his predecessors. The situation is dismal. A "stump" is all that remains of the promise that was to be realized in Jesse's progeny in Isaiah's time. But a bud will eventually blossom and deliver all that was intended by God. This ruler will be spirit-guided. This spirit is not the Third Person of the Blessed Trinity (unimaginable to Isaiah) but rather the force or power of God who accomplishes the divine will effectively and decisively. (Later Christian tradition basing itself on the Septuagint translation of these verses identified in them the seven gifts of the Holy Spirit as known in Christian piety.) Isaiah's conclusion is that there will eventually be a return to paradisiacal circumstances. Peace and harmony between humankind and the animal world will replace the distortions introduced by the first creatures then ratified and continued by their descendants even to our day. It is in truth a declaration that a new creation is possible and will eventually take place. The ideal king will do that because he will rule with justice or righteousness (v. 4).

As scholars point out, Isaiah was not speaking about Jesus but rather about an ideal king who would emerge in the eighth century B.C.E. That Christian tradition and the liturgy use the text to illuminate (not predict) Jesus is part of the way in which our ancestors in the faith (and we) read the Scriptures. The link with the gospel (Matt 3:1-12) is clearly with the

Baptist's declaration that the "mightier" one will judge with the Holy Spirit and fire (vv. 11-12).

## Responsorial Psalm 72:1-2, 7-8, 12-13, 17

This psalm was probably influenced by Isaiah (9:2-7; 11:1-9). It may have been composed for a festival celebrating the anniversary of the ascendance of Hezekiah (714–687 B.C.E.), a king whom Isaiah admired. Since the king actually rules in the place of God, it is well to pray that he rule with justice and fair judgment (vv. 1-2). In a verse not included in today's psalm (14), the king is said to redeem the lives of the poor from oppression and violence. The redeemer in Hebrew society was the next of kin who would rescue relatives from trouble and avenge honor as required. Thus, if the poor are considered kin of the king, and the king rules in place of God, the poor are also kin of God. If a king behaves in this fashion, it is no wonder that his name should be blessed for ever and all the nations acknowledge him.

# Third Sunday of Advent
## Isaiah 35:1-6a, 10

These verses announce a time when God will make significant changes in nature (vv. 1-2) and in human beings (actually in Israel and its sad experience in the prophet's time, vv. 3-4). God will transform arid places (desert, parched land, the steppe) into very fertile land (represented by the most fertile regions of the area: Lebanon, Carmel, Sharon). God will also restore to Israel a vitality that it lost (strengthen, make firm, say "be strong!"). Indeed, God is the reason for this renewed hope: "fear not! Here is your God who will set everything aright." God will replace life denying situations (whether in physical health or in historical experience) with a life-giving and life-enriching context. Isaiah's references to the blind, the deaf, the lame, and mute form the obvious link to today's gospel which alludes to this very passage (Matt 11:4-5).

### Responsorial Psalm 146:6-7, 8-9, 9-10

In this first of a final mini-collection of praise psalms that conclude the Psalter, the psalmist praises God for attending to and taking up residence among the oppressed, hungry, captives, blind, bowed down, strangers (resident aliens), fatherless, the widow—the same category of people mentioned by Isaiah and Matthew. The LORD will be Zion's God forever.

# Fourth Sunday of Advent
*Isaiah 7:10-14*

In the year 734–33 B.C.E. King Ahaz of Judah was unsuccessfully attacked by Israel and Syria. Ahaz had good reason to fear these enemies. He had killed his son, heir to the Davidic throne, and should he be conquered and captured by his enemies, he, too, would be killed. To avoid this, Ahaz asked Tiglath-pilesar of Assyria to rescue him from this danger. Tiglath-pilesar obliged by capturing Damascus, exiling its citizens, and killing its king, Rezin (2 Kgs 16). It is during the time after Ahaz made his request but before Assyria responded that Isaiah approached Ahaz with a message of rescue from God. Ahaz declined to ask a sign from God not out of humility, but rather because he knew he had already secured help from the king of Assyria. Like every prophet, Isaiah speaks God's will for the here and now. His message to Ahaz is: your wife is pregnant, and without the benefit of amniocentesis I can say the child will be a boy. With this heir to replace the one you killed (1 Kgs 16:3), God has assured the continuation of the Davidic line which you have jeopardized. And your ally, Assyria, will shortly capture Israel, the northern kingdom. The birth of this son is the sign that God is with you; hence, you shall name him Emmanuel as a living object lesson for you. In today's gospel, Matthew has inserted these verses into his story of the origins of Jesus.

## Responsorial Psalm 24:1-2, 3-4, 5-6

This highly evolved liturgical psalm contains both ancient vocabulary such as found in Exodus 15 and echoes more re-

6

cent sentiments found in Isaiah and Jeremiah concerning the proper sentiments for approaching the Temple. Who indeed can approach the creator God (vv. 1-2)? One whose hands are sinless, heart is clean, and intention pure (vv. 3-4). The one "who seeks the face of the God of Jacob" (v. 6) will receive a blessing and reward from God the savior. Such a person was Joseph, "a righteous man" (Matt) who stood in stark contrast to Ahaz (Isaiah).

# *Vigil of the Nativity
## *Isaiah 62:1-5*

These verses appear to capture the prophet's meditation on chapters that Second Isaiah, his master, had composed (Isa 40; 51; 54). In these verses Third Isaiah sings about Israel rising to new life from its destruction. The imagery that dominates these verses is drawn from espousals. Zion/Jerusalem's good fortune will break forth as suddenly and brightly as a desert dawn. In antiquity, deities often wore a crown that imitated the walls of their city on earth. Here God is holding such a crown; God is indeed in charge of this glorious restoration. One of the names by which the city once could be described ("forsaken") is the name of a queen mother (*Azuba*–1 Kgs 22:42). Cities were considered to be feminine. The new names carry similar symbolism. For example, "my delight" *(Hephzibah)* is another queen mother (2 Kgs 21:1) but the names portray a reversal of destiny. The forsaken woman (city) is now God's delight. This is especially evident in the name "espoused" *(beᶜula)* which forgets Israel's whoring ways as described by Hosea 2:18.

In this culture, an unfaithful wife would have to be set aside or killed (see Num 5:11-31; Deut 22:13-21). The ideal marriage partner is a patrilateral cousin. What if there is no other available female cousin to replace the unfaithful partner? The man would have to remain unmarried and alone. In the real world of this culture, it is preferable to swallow one's pride, bear the shame, and keep the faithless partner than to be absolutely correct but lose one's partner. So, too, with

8

God. Since all God-talk is based upon and rooted in human experience culturally conditioned, God can be expected to swallow pride, put up with the disappointment, and as the prophet says "as a young man married a virgin, your Builder shall marry you."

The link to the gospel (Matt 1:1-25) is rather clear. Joseph knew Mary was pregnant, and he knew that he was not the father. He would be a thief to claim the child, but Joseph was a holy man who strove to please God always. God's messenger assures Joseph that keeping Mary as spouse is God's plan for him. In Matthew's genealogy, the four women who appear are non-Israelites and some are of dubious character yet each won a place in God's plan. These women possess "acquired honor" thus making Jesus completely honorable since his ancestors in his genealogy possess both ascribed and acquired honor.

### Responsorial Psalm 89:4-5, 16-17, 27, 29

We return again to other verses from this lament. The refrain in particular is a most appropriate response to Third Isaiah's insight. Mention of God's "countenance" brings to mind not only the Temple where Israel went "to see" God but also Moses' experience at Mount Sinai, and other instances which made God's presence very palpable in the mighty deeds God worked for the chosen people. The final verse repeats a familiar adoption formula often sung at the coronation of new kings (see Psalm 2). Indeed, God will remain loyal to this son-king forever; the covenant with him will remain unshaken.

# *Nativity: Midnight Mass
## *Isaiah 9:1-6*

Earlier in the book of Isaiah, we read the prophet's oracle looking for a successor to Ahaz in whom God's promise of a lasting destiny would be realized (Isa 7:14-15). In this chapter, Isaiah describes that successor (possibly Hezekiah, ca. 716 B.C.E.) who ascended to the throne upon his father's death. The first four verses today express hope for deliverance of the northern kingdom. The words "yoke," "pole," and "rod" refer to Assyrian domination even before 721 B.C.E. and hopes that Yahweh would deliver Israel from them. It is difficult for someone who has never lived under an occupying military power to appreciate how conquered people yearn for independence. Anyone who could deliver a nation from such a condition would be a welcome leader.

Verses 5-6 are a triumphant coronation hymn composed by Isaiah for Hezekiah, the son of God's promise in Isaiah 7:14. Wonder-counselor means this king will not need advisers such as those who led his father astray. God-Hero is a mighty warrior designation. Father-Forever describes the quality of his rule, and peace results because of the king's abilities, because God promised it, and because judgment and justice now sustain the dynasty. When Hezekiah did not meet the expectations expressed in these verses and in the previous oracle (7:10-17), Isaiah projected his hopes to a later time (11:1-9). This evening's gospel (Luke 2:1-14) identifies Jesus as the one who fulfills these hopes magnificently: he is Messiah and Lord.

**Responsorial Psalm 96:1-2, 2-3, 11-12, 13**

This is an enthronement psalm that honors God as Israel's king. Today's verses are selected from the first call to praise (vv. 1-3) and the second set of reasons given for this praise (vv. 10-13). The author of this psalm has borrowed heavily from other composers (Psalms 33; 91; 98; and Isa 42:10). The word "announce" (his salvation) is a Hebrew word from which the English word "gospel" derives. This psalmist's inspiration prompts him to broaden the vision of Second Isaiah to a more universal sweep than Isaiah imagined: The Lord shall rule not just Israel but all the earth.

# *Nativity: Mass at Dawn
## *Isaiah 62:11-12*

Third Isaiah seeks to prevent two unfortunate choices in postexilic Jerusalem: that the people will lose hope and settle for less than God has promised, or that they will keep high hopes and become frustrated. These concluding verses of a section proclaiming salvation for a glorious new daughter Zion (Isa 60:1–62:12) string together three uplifting titles: holy people; redeemed of the LORD; and "frequented," that is, a city that is not forgotten but rather visited by its Savior and recognized by all nations. In the accompanying gospel (Luke 2:15-20), after visiting Joseph, Mary, and the infant, the shepherds announce all that had been told to them about Jesus. Third Isaiah's vision for Zion is realized in the birth of Jesus.

### Responsorial Psalm 97:1, 6, 11-12

Another postexilic psalm which honors God as king draws also on other psalms (18; 50; 77) and Second Isaiah. The focus of this psalm and the verses selected for today is justice which in the world of our ancestors in the faith was operative in the realm of patronage, a feature of fictive kinship. A patron is one with surplus who treats clients (needy people) as if they were family, hence, with favoritism. This is how the LORD treats his people (the just, the upright of heart), and all the people will witness this honorable behavior (his glory). The birth of a savior is a gift beyond expectation. Truly such a Patron outshines all others as the refrain reminds us.

# *Nativity: Mass during the Day
## *Isaiah 52:7-10*

Exile is a painful experience. The Polish experience is expressed in the poignant phrase: *żyć na wygnaniu*, "to live somewhere after one was chased out, driven out, banished, expatriated, without rights." The notion involves a sense of belonging and security which is shattered by forced ejection from a sacred place. Without diminishing the historical and cultural uniqueness of each case, perhaps only a person who has experienced an exile can appreciate its reversal.

Today Second Isaiah reports the joy of reversal of the Babylonian Exile but from a strange perspective. It is the watchmen, the ones who did not go into exile, who shout for joy. Scholars note that it was only the elite, the intelligentsia as it were, who were taken away. Ordinary folk remained. Yet both suffered. "How can we sing a song of the LORD in a foreign land?" asked the deportees (Ps 137). Those who did not go into exile had no visionary leaders to lift their spirits or stir their hopes. The best news of all in the prophet's statement is that at last "all the ends of the earth" will see that God is worth believing in. God does care for and remember the people of divine concern. As this reading tells that the people saw God's redemption in progress, the gospel reading for today (John 1:1-18) speaks of Jesus as Word and light giving people the ability to see a new moment in God's redemptive will.

### Responsorial Psalm 98:1, 2-3, 3-4, 5-6

Today's verses drawn from yet another psalm acclaiming God as king of the universe highlight a worldwide participation in the reign of God. Israel is saved, all the nations are witnesses, and the entire physical universe is transformed. Because the Psalm borrows from the first reading ("all the ends of the earth" Ps 98:3–Isa 52:10), it is perfectly suited as a bridge to the gospel and as a link between all the cosmic references in the readings.

# *Sunday within the Octave of Christmas: The Holy Family of Jesus, Mary, and Joseph
## Sirach 3:2-6, 12-14

While today's gospel (Matt 2:13-15, 19-23) highlights Joseph as a responsible husband and father, this first reading focuses on the obligations of sons. Honoring one's father means to submit to the father's will and to remain fiercely loyal to the patriarch. Such a son pleases God who attends to the dutiful son's prayers. Whoever reveres his father will live a long life because the father will not have to kill the disobedient son as God requires (see Deut 21:18-21 about the glutton and drunkard; compare the opinion of people about Jesus in Matt 11:18-19). If one mirror-reads the concluding verses (12-14), that is, imagines the situation that it might plausibly be addressing, one might suspect that disrespect of fathers by sons did occur, perhaps often enough to warrant composition of these verses by the sage. Consider how Jacob at the instigation of his mother Rebecca treated his aged father, Isaac (Gen 27). The prevailing motivation given by the sage for his advice is that God hears the prayers of a dutiful and honorable son. Considering the concern God shows toward Joseph in today's gospel, it is plausible to conclude that Joseph was an honorable son who revered his own father. When faced with challenges in his own married life, Joseph turned in prayer to God who responded favorably as the gospel indicates.

## Responsorial Psalm 128:1-2, 3, 4-5

This psalm highlights the blessings that come to a person who fears the LORD. The word fear does not describe an emotion that causes trembling, or the knees to weaken, and the like. It rather describes an awareness of who God is and how one relates to God. Acknowledging that the creature is not God will gain for the creature God's blessings in labor, in the family circle, and in all of Israel. In this case, the blessings are a fertile wife and many, presumably obedient, children.

# *January 1 Octave Day of Christmas: Solemnity of the Blessed Virgin Mary, the Mother of God
*Numbers 6:22-27*

Many Christians recognize these verses as the Blessing of St. Francis written by him for Brother Leo who requested a special, personal benediction. Others may recall that these verses form the traditional conclusion to the Synagogue Sabbath service. In the context of the Hebrew Bible, these verses emphasize the "face" of God and hearken back to the experience of Moses himself: "The LORD used to speak to Moses face to face, as one man speaks to another" (Exod 33:11). In this respect Moses was considered to be unique among all the prophets: "Since then no prophet has arisen in Israel like Moses, whom the LORD knew face to face" (Deut 34:10). But what of the persistent biblical tradition that no human being could survive such a face to face encounter with God: "But my face you cannot see, for no man sees me and still lives" (Exod 33:20)? The text does not say that such a vision is impossible, only that it can be fatal. That is why people who survive can express only awe and wonder. ". . . I have seen God face to face . . . yet my life has been spared," marveled Jacob (Gen 32:31).

In Israel, the verses from Numbers had been used as a priestly blessing from very early times during the three feasts

(Passover, Pentecost, Tabernacles) when Israelites went to present themselves to the Lord to "see his face." Thus the phrase meant going on pilgrimage to the Temple in Jerusalem. The priestly verses, then, expressed the confident hope that those who came to experience God in the Temple would not be disappointed. The gospel (Luke 2:16-21) reports the responses of some who had met Jesus face to face: the shepherds went and told others; Mary pondered these things in her heart. How would you respond to a face to face meeting with God or the risen Jesus?

### Responsorial Psalm 67:2-3, 5, 6, 8

Originally this psalm may have been a non-Israelite statement of gratitude for a bountiful harvest. Appending the priestly prayer in the opening verses would have accommodated it to the Israelite tradition. When God displays the divine "face" (= self), God manifests personal delight and gracious generosity. This is God's way of dealing with human beings (vv. 2-3). Nations should rejoice (vv. 5, 6) and so should all the earth (v. 8). God deals with human beings justly, as a father deals with family members. The final verse "all the ends of the earth" (which has yielded its increase) is a fitting reference to Mary, since Jesus, the fruit of her womb, is part of this earth's "yield" (see Gal 4:4 which is the second reading for today; and relate also to today's gospel). These psalm verses make a fitting bridge between all three readings.

# *Second Sunday after Christmas
### *Sirach 24:1-2, 8-12*

Known as the "Praise of Wisdom," this poem (24:1-33) begins the second major division of Sirach (24–50). Today's
verses are drawn from a twenty-two-line speech delivered
by Wisdom in the first person (vv. 3-17, 19-22). The author
introduces Wisdom in verses 1 and 2. By themselves, these
verses do indeed indicate the honorable status of Wisdom,
but both to modern and especially ancient ears, they are in-
complete without verse 3. Modern listeners might repeat
the folk-adage, "self-praise stinks." Ancient Mediterranean
listeners would bristle to hear someone speak without humility, that is, without deliberately putting oneself down a notch
or two so that others can raise one up to one's proper status.
Verse 3 explains why the first two verses are culturally appropriate: Wisdom came from the mouth of the Most High. This
explains the respect and reputation she enjoys in the assembly of the Most high, in the midst of her people, and in the
multitude of the chosen.

Twenty-two lines imitate an acrostic poem, that is, one in
which each line begins with a successive letter of the Hebrew
alphabet. This speech is not an acrostic. The final verses of
today's reading (8-12) tell us that God commanded Wisdom
to dwell in Israel because she was unable to find a suitable
place elsewhere on earth by a personal search. Dwelling in
the "tent" is an allusion to the dwelling that God commanded
Moses to build (Exod 25:8-19; 26:1-37). That she ministers

there suggests that Wisdom as Law laid down the liturgical rules to be followed in the worship of the Lord. She continued when the Temple replaced the tent, and she remains ever present among God's people. Reference to Wisdom (spoken by God) living in a tent (24:8) links nicely with the statement in today's gospel that "God's word became human and [literally in Greek] pitched its tent among us" (John 1:14).

## Responsorial Psalm 147:12-13, 14-15, 19-20

These verses are drawn from the three quasi-independent hymns that constitute this psalm: vv. 1-6; 7-11; and 12-20 which focus on God as Lord of Zion through the creative word. Mention of Zion and repetition of various synonyms for word—command, statutes, ordinances—demonstrate how these verses serve as a suitable bridge between the first reading and the gospel. Indeed, the refrain makes that explicit: "The Word of God became man and lived among us."

# *January 6: Epiphany
## *Isaiah 60:1-6*

Third Isaiah speaks a word of encouragement to the residents of Jerusalem. To offset the discouragement deriving from the trickle of returnees from exile, the prophet uses the "prophetic perfect" tense (v. 1: light has come, glory shines [has shone]) which firmly declares that salvation is still to come. An action initiated in the past is yet to be completed. Paltry beginnings should not discourage anyone. God lights up the Holy City which invites all to gather and come (vv. 1-3). The imagery stirs hope. First the scattered deportees of Israel return ("your sons . . . and daughters"). Then come the non-Israelites from far away. "Riches of the sea" would indicate the region north to Tyre and Phoenicia; "Midian and Ephah" point to the region south to the Arabian desert and east to the Gulf of Aqabah; "Sheba" refers to south Arabia. Some scholars think Matthew in today's gospel (2:1-12) drew inspiration from these verses of Isaiah when he mentions gold and frankincense. The passage has long been associated with the feast of the Epiphany in the liturgy.

### Responsorial Psalm 72:1-2, 7-8, 10-11, 12-13

Traces of Isaiah 9:2-7 and 11:1-9 in this psalm support the opinion that it was composed in honor of King Hezekiah (715–687 B.C.E.) with verse 10 added still later (compare Isa 60:6-10). Today's verses praise the ideal kin-person's justice and judgment (1-2). He shall establish peace over the ideal expanse of Israel: from the Red Sea to the Mediterranean, from the desert to the Euphrates ("sea to sea," vv. 7-8). The psalmist pushes the boundaries even to Spain (Tarshish) and Ethiopia (Seba, vv. 10-11)! Why should this king's empire extend so far? Because he will vindicate the lowly, poor, and afflicted (vv. 12-13). Yes, as the refrain indicates, every nation can admire such a ruler.

# *Baptism of the Lord
# (First Sunday in Ordinary Time)
## *Isaiah 42:1-4, 6-7*

These verses are commonly identified as one of the four "Servant" songs in Isaiah (42:1-4; 49:1-6; 50:4-9a; 52:13–53:12). Current scholarship suggests that they were an integral part of Second Isaiah (40–55) from the beginning and were not later additions. The Servant is Israel presented as a collectivistic individual. At the present time, approximately 90 percent of the world's population are collectivistic individuals. Such people stand in sharp contrast to individuals as they are known in Western cultures (representing just 10 percent of the world's population). Collectivistic personalities draw their identity from the group (nation; family) and do not want to stand out from the crowd. While earlier biblical scholarship talked about corporate personality, it is more appropriate today to speak of collectivistic personalities. Thus, while these Servant Songs in Isaiah sound as if they are describing a specific individual, they really describe the nation. Any individual member of this nation would readily identify with the description.

These particular verses deal with the destiny of the Servant. Above all, the Servant will reveal and establish justice or God's law, to all the nations. The Servant will teach everything that is needed for leading a well-ordered life pleasing to God. Israel will not assume the posture of an arrogant and rushing victor but will rather offer a living example of obedience to God's will. In this way will she be a light to the nations. One basic link between this reading and the gospel (Matt 3:13-17) is the notion of someone with whom God is pleased: the Servant and Jesus. What kind of job description would you write for such a person?

## Responsorial Psalm 29:1-2, 3-4, 3, 9-10

This hymn was borrowed from Canaanite culture where it was sung in honor of Baal, god of thunder and conqueror of the mighty waters. The Israelites substituted "voice of the LORD" for "voice of Baal" and repeated it seven times while singing this hymn in the liturgical assembly. Of course, thunder is the voice of the LORD, and these psalm verses point to today's gospel reading in which the sky is torn open and the voice from the sky says of Jesus: "This is my beloved Son, with whom I am well pleased."

# Second Sunday in Ordinary Time
*Isaiah 49:3, 5-6*

This second of the four Servant Songs in Isaiah identifies Israel as the Servant (v. 3). In verse 5, however, the Servant's mission is to Israel, to bring it back from exile and gather it to Yahweh. Scholars admit that it is futile to attempt to identify this Servant as a historical personage. He may well have been, but the evidence in the Songs is difficult if not impossible to attach to any known person. It is best to concentrate on the ideas in the songs. In today's few verses, Servant's specific task is identified: he is to end the Exile and lead Israel back home (v. 6: raise up and restore). Indeed, his task is to be a light and salvation to Israelites scattered among the nations beyond Babylon and lead them back to the homeland. Given the ethnocentric and exclusivistic perspectives of ancient Israelites and the particularistic concerns of Yahweh their God as recorded in the tradition, it is difficult to imagine how and why this would appeal to non-Israelites, "the ends of the earth." The alternative interpretation, that Isaiah presents Yahweh as interested in non-Israelites, is quite likely the reason why these verses were selected to be paired with the gospel in which Jesus "takes away the sin of the world" (John 1:29). Yet in John, "world" is explicitly associated with Israel and Israelites (see John 18:20: "I have spoken openly to the world; I have always taught in synagogues, and in the temple where all the Jews come together").

## Responsorial Psalm 40:2, 4, 7-8, 8-9, 10

Waiting in the Bible often implies that a very difficult and sad time is nearly ended. The Hebrew literally ("waited I waited") expresses the sentiment emphatically. The wait was worth it, for God caused the petitioner to sing again. Verses 7-8 describe the variety of ritual acts which one could experience or perform in the Temple, but the psalmist highlights instead his obedient attention to God's will, itself a gift of God to him. This in fact is the refrain in today's responsorial psalm. The psalmist has so integrated God's Law/will into his very being that he not only executes it but announces God's justice openly and boldly.

# Third Sunday
# in Ordinary Time
## *Isaiah 8:23–9:3*

This oracle contrasts the sad state of affairs under Ahaz with the complete reversal under his son-successor, Hezekiah. Oppression by the Assyrian empire is challenged and defeated through brutal military action in which the arms of the enemy soldiers are destroyed (compare Ps 46:8-9). It is of course Yahweh who works this victory through the agency of a new David. Thus is darkness replaced by light. Rejoicing is the only natural response, rejoicing as at the harvest when the crops are finally gathered safe from threatening weather conditions or as at the definitive conquest and humiliation of an enemy. The link with today's gospel (Matt 4:12-23) is that the evangelist cites these verses of Isaiah to characterize Jesus as that "great light" when he moves to Capernaum "in the region of Zebulun and Naphtali" to begin his ministry.

### Responsorial Psalm 27:1, 4, 13-14

The Temple dominates these verses selected from the section of this psalm that expresses confident trust in God. Light is associated with life in the biblical tradition, hence the refrain which is drawn from verse 1 (the LORD and my salvation) repeats that association to highlight the psalmist's confidence. He longs to be with the God in his Temple and to enjoy rescue from his predicaments and the enjoyment of full life. This is reason to wait patiently if longingly.

# Fourth Sunday
# in Ordinary Time
*Zephaniah 2:3; 3:12-13*

Zephaniah prophesied in the days of Josiah (640–609 B.C.E.) who promoted reform during his reign. Indeed, Zephaniah may have played a role early in Josiah's reform movement. Judah was a vassal of Assyria after its northern neighbor, Israel, fell to that empire. At this time about a century later, Assyria is weakening and Egypt seeks to extend its own power while propping up Assyria against Babylon, rising on the political horizon. Zephaniah's basic message is that God will destroy Assyria, punish the chosen people for their infidelities, but draw from these a reformed, more pleasing group of people.

Today's verses describe the kind of people who appeal to God: the humble *(anawim)*, those who observe God's law, seek justice and humility. Such will do no wrong nor engage in lying and deceit. This is quite a radical expectation since deception and lying have ever been legitimate strategies in the Middle East for defending one's reputation, one's honor. Yet, if this faithful remnant can adopt this lifestyle pleasing to God, they will enjoy secure peace. In today's gospel (Matt 5:1-12a), Jesus fleshes out these characteristics of those who find favor with God.

### Responsorial Psalm 146:6-7, 8-9, 9-10

In this first of a final mini-collection of praise psalms that conclude the Psalter, the psalmist praises God for attending to and taking up residence among the oppressed, hungry, captives, blind, bowed down, strangers (resident aliens), fatherless, the widow—the same category of people mentioned by Isaiah and Matthew. The LORD will be Zion's God forever.

# Fifth Sunday
# in Ordinary Time
*Isaiah 58:7-10*

Peasants are notoriously yet understandably selfish. Living at subsistence levels, not knowing where the next meal is coming from, a peasant has little choice but to hoard and look out for the family above everyone else. The imperatives in this text segment from Third Isaiah are aimed not at selfish individualists but rather selfish collectivistic personalities who place the welfare of their small and personal group ahead of all other groups, especially those of fellow Israelites (v. 7, "turn your back on your own"). The experience of Assyrian domination quite likely heightened these peasant tendencies. Through Isaiah, God bargains with the people. "If" you feed the hungry, care for the afflicted, etc., etc., "then" when you need my help, says God, I will reply: "Here I am!" In particular, "light" (a faithful Davidic king) will rise in the "darkness" (Assyrian domination), and all will be well. The link with the gospel (Matt 5:13-16) is probably the word "light." It's not clear that the architects of the Lectionary intended more than that superficial correspondence of a single word. Even so, just as Israelites are to "light fires" (stimulate discussion) among fellow Israelites by challenging selfish behaviors, so too are Jesus' disciples to light similar fires by their behavior so as to become "light of the world."

## Responsorial Psalm 112:4-5, 6-7, 8-9

This acrostic psalm (each half verse begins with a successive letter of the Hebrew alphabet) seeks to promote covenant loyalty and describes the just person. This is the kind of person described by Isaiah and by Jesus (salt of the earth). Such a one is indeed "light in darkness to the upright."

# Sixth Sunday in Ordinary Time
## Sirach 15:15-20

Echoing Deuteronomy 11:26-28 and 30:15-20, Sirach extolls human free choice (he repeats the word "choose" three times in this text segment). Human beings are faced with choices: fire and water, life and death, good and evil, and everything in between these extremes which are, in general, synonymous. God forces no human being to anything, yet because of this freedom God cannot be said to give "license to sin." The basic choice is to keep the commandments and trust, that is, remain unswervingly loyal to God. "Commandments" is the notion that links this reading with today's gospel (Matt 5:17-37) where Jesus expands the thrust of some commandments. Yet he promises that the one who keeps and teaches them "will be called greatest in the kingdom of heaven."

### Responsorial Psalm 119:1-2, 4-5, 17-18, 33-34

This longest psalm in the Psalter is both structured (an alphabetical psalm) and unstructured (thematically jumbled) in composition. In general, the psalmist uses eight synonyms for law. Today's verses report these synonyms: decrees, precepts, statutes, and words. The reward for following the Law of the Lord is to be truly blessed, honorable, esteemed, and rewarded by God the author of these commandments.

# Seventh Sunday in Ordinary Time
*Leviticus 19:1-2, 17-18*

At least five times in Leviticus the Israelites are exhorted to be holy because the LORD is holy. The word holy means to be set apart exclusively, in these instances for the God of Israel. Verses 17 and 18 describe very explicitly who these "set apart" people are, and how one ought to comport with them. Specifically, this people set apart are one's neighbor (v. 18), one's brother (v. 17; sister is not in the Hebrew text; the Hebrew word for brother is not inclusive), a fellow citizen, fellow countryman, member of one's own people. Love in this passage is quite circumscribed: it is restricted to one's own kind. The Lukan Jesus, of course, changes this in Luke 10:25-37. The link to the gospel (Matt 5:38-48) is Jesus' allusion to Leviticus 19:18 with his addition of a phrase found nowhere in the Hebrew Bible: "hate your enemy." (Jesus may have been reporting a common understanding and interpretation of Lev 19:18 with this added phrase.) In addition, Matthew's Jesus had reformulated the exhortation "be holy" to "be perfect, just as your heavenly Father is perfect" (v. 48).

### Responsorial Psalm 103:1-2, 3-4, 8, 10, 12-13

The psalmist is grateful to God for restored health (v. 3) and his sentiments of indebtedness for this gift eventually become a hymn of praise. The LORD is merciful, gracious, slow to anger, kind, forgiving, and compassionate to "those who fear him." In that last phrase lies the key to obtaining God's favor. It is this same God whom Jesus describes as making the sun rise on the bad and good, and the rain to fall on the just and unjust.

# Eighth Sunday in Ordinary Time
## Isaiah 49:14-15

One theme pervades Isaiah 49:13-16: Yahweh's loyalty to the chosen people will bring an end to exile and restore them to Jerusalem. Israel cannot see beyond its present moment of despondence and concludes that the LORD has forsaken and forgotten it. This is its lament in verse 14. Yahweh's response is phrased in terms familiar to all human beings. Though in general mothers bond closely with their children and care for them tenderly, human experience knows of mothers who do indeed neglect or abandon their children. It is sad and tragic, but it does happen. Yahweh's behavior contrasts with this exception. Yahweh will never forget Israel, its child. The obvious link with today's gospel (Matt 6:24-34) is Jesus' insistence that God will faithfully provide the necessities of life and more.

### Responsorial Psalm 62:2-3, 6-7, 8-9

The verses drawn from this psalm capture its sentiments masterfully. The psalmist is at peace, confident that God remains faithful to him. Three times God is called "rock," a title very likely inspired by the rock on which the Temple stood. Twice God is identified as "my salvation, my stronghold." The psalmist affirms: "I shall not be disturbed at all." These verses serve as a perfect bridge between the first reading in which Israel as a nation feels abandoned by God, and the gospel in which Jesus addresses peasants who lived at a level of marginal subsistence and reminds them that God will take care of the necessities of life (food, clothing). The reminder is certainly valid for all cultures and all generations.

# Ninth Sunday in Ordinary Time
*Deuteronomy 11:18, 26-28*

This reading and the gospel are linked by a focus on "words" (of God; and of Jesus). In Middle Eastern cultures, it is acceptable to say the right thing even if one does not intend to act upon it. The son who had no intention of working in his father's vineyard yet assured the father that he would is a good example (Matt 21:30). Here in Deuteronomy, Yahweh demands obedience and rewards it with blessings. Lest the person forget God's words, Yahweh instructs them to bind the words at the wrist and on the forehead (see also Deut 6:8; Exod 13:9, 16). This gave rise to the use of phylacteries (Hebrew: *tefillin*) in the Second Temple period (see Matt 23:5). More importantly, the believer is exhorted to internalize God's words and to act upon them. In the gospel (Matt 7:21-27), Jesus challenges the Middle Eastern cultural value of spontaneously saying what the other person expects to hear. Instead, he insists that those who hear his words also put them into practice.

### Responsorial Psalm 31:2-3, 3-4, 17, 25

The late Father Carroll Stuhlmueller observed that this psalm borrows heavily from other parts of the Bible (notably Psalms and Jeremiah). Yet the psalmist is not a plagiarist. He breathes fresh life into the verses he borrows and gives them new context. He is definitely a person who has not simply listened to words but internalized and lived them in his distinctive circumstances. He knows God intimately. In the phrase "for your name's sake," name is a synonym for person. The psalmist is so personally convinced of God's assistance that he exhorts his listeners to similar confidence.

# Tenth Sunday in Ordinary Time
*Hosea 6:3-6*

The Matthean Jesus cites Hosea (according to the Septuagint) in today's gospel (Matt 9:9-13). This is the link between the readings. In addressing his eighth century B.C.E. audience, the prophet Hosea presents Yahweh's scorn for the purely external worship rituals Israel observes without actually obeying Yahweh's commands. Israel's piety is evanescent like the dew which evaporates with the rising of the sun. Though it seeks to repent, Israel's repentance is not deep rooted nor lasting. Therefore God's judgment will come as surely as the spring rain. God will not relent.

### Responsorial Psalm 50:1, 8, 12-13, 14-15

Very likely originating before the Exile in a period of well being, these verses are not really critical of sacrifice. God doesn't need any of them. What God desires above all is praise, that is, honor, recognition of and respect for divine status. This is quite in line with the core Mediterranean cultural values. This kind of behavior will obtain from God rescue from distress which, in its turn, should prompt the recipient to further glorify or honor God.

# First Sunday of Lent
*Genesis 2:7-9; 3:1-7*

The Old Testament readings for the Sundays of Lent present highlights from the history of God's salvific dealings with humanity. Today's reading relates that part of the creation myth from Israel's prehistory which describes the transgression of the first creatures against a specific command by God concerning the tree of the knowledge of good and evil (Gen 2:16). It is significant to note that this prohibition was given before the woman was created (Gen 2:21-22), for the tempter appears to focus only on the woman (Gen 3:1-7). How did she learn the command? Why did the serpent misrepresent the command? What prompted the woman to similarly misrepresent the command by expanding it ("or even touch it," Gen 3:3)? Why is her husband silent during her conversation with the serpent? Why does he acquiesce to his partner's offer of the fruit without raising any caution or objection?

Scholars propose a variety of answers to the above questions, but the bottom line is that both creatures disobeyed God's command and paid the penalty: "death." It is important to recognize that this word does not mean physical death. They did not drop dead upon eating the fruit. Rather they cut themselves off from intimate communion with God (see Ezekiel 18). God confirms that decision by driving them from the garden and the remaining "temptation," namely, to eat of the tree of life and thus gain immortality. The link between this reading and the gospel (Matt 4:1-11) is the idea of testing loyalty. The first creatures proved disloyal to God; Jesus remains perfectly loyal to the Father.

**Responsorial Psalm 51:3-4, 5-6, 12-13, 17**

This is very likely one of the best known of the seven penitential psalms (Pss 6; 32; 38; 51; 102; 130; 143). It is best dated between 537 B.C.E. (end of the Exile) and 445 B.C.E. (the rebuilding of Jerusalem's walls). The verses selected for today contain some of the rich vocabulary for sin and forgiveness. From a Mediterranean cultural perspective, to sin against God is to shame God. Shame requires revenge (see Leviticus 26 for the kind of punishment God will mete out for being shamed). The psalmist, however, is confident God will do what other Mediterranean human beings sometimes do, namely, forego revenge and show mercy instead (see Matt 18:15-35). If God shows mercy, the psalmist will proclaim God's praise, that is God's truly honorable reputation as merciful and compassionate when God has every right to be vindictive.

# Second Sunday of Lent
*Genesis 12:1-4a*

The common bond between this reading and the gospel (Matt 17:1-9) is that each is a report of an experience of God in an altered state of consciousness, God's customary way of communicating with creatures (see 1 Sam 3:1). Of course, in each reading the content of God's communication differs. In this report God personally directs Abraham to leave his native land (Ur, located on the Euphrates River in the southern portion of Mesopotamia—modern Iraq) and settle in Haran far to the North (on the Balikh river in upper Mesopotamia—modern Turkey). Haran, however, a major caravan center at this period, is only the beginning of Abraham's journey to land God will show him. The trip will continue to Shechem, Bethel, and the Negeb.

Verses 2-3 express seven blessings (the word appears five times, two specific blessings—great nation, great name—bring the number to seven), and itself is the first of seven reports of blessings which end in Genesis 22:16-18 (which also contains seven expressions of blessing). Since seven symbolizes perfection, Abraham will indeed be completely blessed by God.

## Responsorial Psalm 33:4-5, 18-19, 20, 22

This psalm of praise celebrates the creative power of the word (v. 4) which is an idea that was common in the sacred writings of Egypt and Babylon as it was in ancient Israel. Indeed, "word" and "works" stand in parallelism in verse 4: the divine word is personal, effective, dependable. Further,

God watches ("eye of the LORD," v. 18) over those who fear him to come to their rescue as they have need of it. The concluding verses pray that God remain faithful in extending steadfast loving-kindness (Hebrew: *ḥesed* translated by the Greek word for "mercy" as reflected in the refrain).

# Third Sunday of Lent
*Exodus 17:3-7*

Quite likely the reference to water links this reading to today's gospel (John 4:5-42). This reading reports the third of ten "tests of loyalty (= faith)" that God directs to the people freed from Egypt. The people have no water to drink at all, so they attack Moses. Are they to die of thirst here, thanks to following him out of Egypt? Moses in his turn directs their complaint to God. After all, their complaint amounts to saying that they doubt God can provide water for them in the wilderness. The people thus test God in their turn. Surprisingly, God does not rebuke anyone for this challenge to the divine reputation. Instead, God tells Moses how to provide water for the people to drink. The root of the place name Meriba is *rib,* which means "to quarrel." That word also describes the "lawsuit" pattern (between Yahweh and the people), a literary form popular among the Prophets. Massa derives from the Hebrew verb *nissa* meaning "to test." At this place of testing, God successfully provided water for the people thus proving that indeed, God is in their midst.

## Responsorial Psalm 95:1-2, 6-7, 8-9

This psalm reflects the influence of Deuteronomy and Second Isaiah, both associated with the old kingdom of Israel. Indeed, repetition of the word "today" (day; this day) characterizes Deuteronomy (4:30; 5:3; 6:1; 7:11; etc.). References to God as creator of the universe and shepherd of Israel occur often in Second Isaiah (40:11; 41:21-24; etc.).

The psalmist's references to Massah and Meriba make this a fitting response to the reading from Exodus and appropriate bridge to the gospel report situated at Jacob's well in Sychar.

# Fourth Sunday of Lent
*1 Samuel 16:1b, 6-7, 10-13a*

This story that reports the selection of David as God's choice to succeed Saul as king contains a very important cultural insight. "Not as man sees does God see, because man sees the appearance but the LORD looks into the heart" (1 Sam 16:7). Middle Eastern people of antiquity and the present day are not only non-introspective but anti-introspective. The cultural belief is exactly as is stated here. Humans do not have the ability to read hearts, to get to know other human beings very well. They can only judge by externals, which is a central feature of honor, or claims to worth, value, reputation. This core culture Middle Eastern value is based entirely on appearances, on how one can make oneself out to be, and how that appearance would be perceived and judged by others. In other words, psychology and psychological analysis, so dear to Western readers of the Bible, is of little to no use in understanding and interpreting characters in the Bible.

Only God can read hearts, can know the truth about human beings. This insight is also important for understanding Jesus as presented in the New Testament. He frequently is said to know what other people are thinking (Mark 2:6-8; 9:33-34; John 2:24-25; 16:19, 30). The late eminent American biblical scholar Fr. Raymond Brown noted that statements of this nature seem to be secondary theological modifications. In general, the Gospel tradition does not hesitate to report normal ignorance on Jesus' part of the ordinary affairs of life (e.g., Mark 5:30-33 or Luke 2:52).

Cultural insight can sharpen Fr. Brown's observations. All cultures recognize a kind of person whom they identify as a "holy man" (or "holy woman"). Siberian Tungus call such a person a shaman, a word that should not be applied to similar figures outside that culture. A holy person has direct contact with God, intercedes on behalf of other human beings, and is especially blessed by God with gifts of healing. Prophets in the Israelite tradition fit the description of holy man/holy woman. So too does Jesus. In fact, it is the very first title attributed to him in the gospel tradition: "I know who you are," shouted out an unclean spirit, "the Holy One of God" (Mark 1:24).

In today's reading, God communicates with the prophet, Samuel, to inform him of the divine choice of a successor to Saul, namely, David: "There—anoint him, for this is the one!"

### Responsorial Psalm 23:1-3a, 3b-4, 5, 6

This psalm is a fitting response to the first reading in which God selects a shepherd to be a successor to King Saul. Indeed, the psalm highlights that God is fully in charge: he leads the psalmist, guides him in right paths, protects him against dangers, enables him to partake of the family banquet [in the sight of his enemies] that customarily followed the thanksgiving sacrifice in the Temple. The psalmist concludes confidently that he will dwell forever in the Promised Land to enjoy every opportunity to participate in Temple services, undisturbed. Though the healed blind man in today's gospel is thrown out by the authorities (John 9:34), Jesus has rescued him from his malady and accepts him as a believer.

# Fifth Sunday of Lent
*Ezekiel 37:12-14*

These are the concluding verses of Ezekiel's vision of "dry bones," that is, dead Israel. Verses 2-20 report the vision, while verses 11-14 interpret the vision. This follows the pattern of all vision experiences, all altered states of consciousness experiences. The visionary sees things in disjointed, that is, nonlinear fashion. The interpretation involves putting some order into the vision and interpreting it.

Ezekiel's prophetic message is that God will restore new life to Israel conquered (killed) by the Babylonians and taken into exile. "Spirit" which alternatively means the wind, breath, spirit of God, figures prominently in the entire text segment (vv. 1, 5, 6, 8, 9, 10, 14). Clearly the prophet uses this as his major interpretive concept. The main point of Ezekiel's vision/message is that it is none other than God's very own spirit that will restore life to Israel. The link between this reading and the gospel is clearly life, or more precisely, restoration to life (Israel in Ezekiel; Lazarus in John).

### Responsorial Psalm 130:1-2, 3-4, 5-6, 7-8

This is the sixth of the seven penitential psalms. Traditionally identified as an individual lament, this psalm—like all others in this category—is the lament of a collectivistic personality who takes his identity from the group and can never consider him or herself as distinct from the group. Thus all the "I" verses slip quite smoothly into the collectivity, Israel, in verse 6 and conclude there in verse 7. Understanding and appreciating this concept is challenging for Western, individualistic readers of the Bible. Nevertheless, it is critically important for appreciating our ancestors in faith. The notion is clear in Ezekiel (bones of Israel) and in John (Lazarus will rise in the resurrection of all on the last day).

# *Palm Sunday of the Lord's Passion
## *Isaiah 50:4-7*

Just like the other Servant Songs, this third in the series of
four from Second Isaiah describes the nation Israel in history
and in Captivity. She will recognize herself in the persecuted,
suffering, sick person, just as Isaiah (1:4, 6) described: "Ah,
sinful nation, people laden with wickedness. . . . From the
sole of the foot to the head there is no sound spot . . ." The
very last verses of today's text segment are especially noteworthy. The Lord God is my help; I am not disgraced. The
apparently shameful appearance and behavior of this servant
is not really shameful if God is on his side. It is important for
a male to defend his honor at all costs. But if a male finds
himself in a losing situation such as being forced to go to
court which is a definite no-win situation, then the male's
honorable behavior is to endure the worst without flinching
or crying. The honorable aspect of what seems to be shameful behavior, of course, is the notion that Mark's Passion
story in its entirety (Palm Sunday and Easter Vigil gospel
reading together) fleshes out for Jesus. While Jesus seemed to
be irredeemably shamed in the betrayal, trial, crucifixion,
death, and burial in a stranger's tomb, God raised him from
the dead. God must have been very pleased with Jesus to
honor him in this way.

### Responsorial Psalm 22:8-9, 17-18, 19-20, 23-24

This lament of a person who suffers unjustly but patiently
is quoted thirteen times in the New Testament and nine times

alone in the Passion story. The psalmist is not complaining, shows no bitterness, makes no allusion to sin, does not declare personal innocence, and makes no defense against unjust charges. The suffering petitioner simply places himself entirely in the hands of God. In this he finds great peace.

The first segment (vv. 8-9) reports the shameful taunts, the inhuman ridicule. The next segment literally claims that persecutors have mauled his hands and feet as would a lion (vv. 17-18). The petitioner beseeches God to hear his prayer (vv. 19-20). The final segment that announces a public expression of grateful indebtedness in the assembly testifies to the fact that God came to the rescue (vv. 23-24).

# The Triduum

For commentary on the Old Testament readings of the Triduum, see John J. Pilch, *The Triduum and Easter Sunday: Breaking Open the Scripture* (Collegeville: Liturgical Press, 2000).

# *Easter Sunday
*Acts 10:34a, 37-43*

To appreciate the readings of Easter time, it is helpful to understand a common human experience known as altered states of consciousness that are different from "normal" or "ordinary" consciousness. Brain and nervous system research indicates all human beings are capable of such experiences. Indeed, many are familiar with daydreaming, road trance (hypnosis while driving, yet obeying all laws and arriving at one's destination safely, etc.), and similar altered states. Cultures give distinctive interpretations to such experiences, but some cultures are reluctant to acknowledge them as healthy elements of human experience. Psychiatric research indicates that in some cultures, people can expect to see their deceased loves ones in an altered state of consciousness for as long as ten years after the death, and sometimes longer. Anthropological studies recount that altered states of consciousness experiences are common in the circum-Mediterranean world of the present and of the past.

Peter delivers his speech within the context of his experience with Cornelius, a centurion of the Italian Cohort (Acts 10:1–11:18). In ecstatic trance, Cornelius is instructed to seek out Peter and Peter, also in ecstatic trance, is instructed by God that all foods are clean. When Cornelius personally repeats his experience to Peter, Peter makes a speech, some verses of which have been selected for today's reading.

Of interest to our reflection is Peter's report about experiencing the risen Jesus. Peter notes that "God granted that he be visible, not to all the people, but to us." Of course, God is the one who "hard-wired" human beings with the capacity for varieties of consciousness, and God can also select the subjects of specific experiences. Sometimes God can even communicate with "enemies" in an altered state of consciousness (e.g., Nebuchadnezzar in Dan 2). While all human beings are indeed capable of the experience, the experiences will always be individual and culture specific.

Peter also observes that they ate and drank with the risen Jesus. This is not a literary device but rather the report of an actual experience. The Israelite tradition believed that holy men *(ṣaddiq; ḥasid)* would eat at three-legged golden tables overflowing with delicacies in "the world to come." In the Israelite tradition, this phrase, "the world to come" points to that place where the righteous will go after they die and depart from "this world." Psychological anthropologists would call that world "alternate reality," in contrast to this world which is ordinary reality, or culturally "normal" reality. Thus some experiences in altered states of consciousness are experiences of alternate reality, including "the world to come" which is parallel to ordinary reality, or as the Israelite tradition calls it, "this world."

Finally, Peter reports the consequences of seeing the risen Jesus in an altered state of consciousness. The apostles were commissioned to preach and testify to Jesus as appointed by God to judge the living and the dead. Anthropologists observed that two common results of alternate states of consciousness experiences are (1) the visionary finds a solution to a problem, or (2) is strengthened to embark on a new path in life. Clearly Peter and the apostles experienced the second effect. This reading from Acts relates well with the gospel (John 20:1-9) in which Mary of Magdala, Simon Peter, and the other disciple find the empty tomb but do not yet experience the risen Jesus. It is the normal, first stage of experience after the death of a loved one.

### Responsorial Psalm 118:1-2, 16-17, 22-23

This is an entrance psalm from a Temple liturgy perhaps at a "Gate of Righteousness" which is offering solemn gratitude to God. The psalm also appears to have been associated with pilgrimages to Jerusalem on the feast of Tabernacles. It was an integral part of the Passover celebration recited in conjunction with filling the fourth cup of wine. The first two verses initiate the communal statement of grateful indebtedness. Verses 16-17 echo Moses' song in Exodus 15, while the final verses (22-23) are quite likely an ancient proverb highlighting the difference that faith or loyalty can make. One person's junk becomes another person's treasure by faith. The late Fr. Carroll Stuhlmueller suggested that the psalm refrain (v. 24) "this is the day the Lord has made" is better translated "on the day when the Lord takes action." Indeed, on that day, Jesus was raised from the dead.

# Second Sunday of Easter
*Acts 2:42-47*

Scholars are generally agreed that these verses, like other such summaries in Acts, paint an ideal picture. Luke's intent is to depict a "golden age," a utopia as it were, similar to Hellenistic traditions about "origins" and political utopias. True, there is likely some basis in reality of the Christian community for this reflection, but in general the report still remains an idealization as the subsequent story about Ananias and Sapphira indicates (5:1-11). The "communal life" (v. 42) to which the believers committed themselves included common activities such as teaching, praying, worshiping, working of mighty deeds ("wonders and signs"), and almsgiving. In this last mentioned activity, it is noteworthy that the community shared "among all according to each one's need." Luke's Jesus seemed to call for more than this: "In the same way, everyone of you who does not renounce all his possessions cannot be my disciple" (Luke 14:33).

### Responsorial Psalm 118:2-4, 13-15, 22-24

The refrain of this psalm which echoes vv. 1-4 hymns God's unswerving loyalty (steadfast-love; mercy) toward a person who was in dire straits ("hard pressed" and "falling"). Verses 22-24 are interpreted variously in the New Testament, and each case must be viewed in its context. In today's liturgy, the association of these verses with Jesus' death (and resurrection) reflects Mark's use of them (12:10-12).

# Third Sunday of Easter
*Acts 2:14, 22-33*

In this part of Peter's speech after the Pentecost event, he addresses fellow members of the house of Israel exclusively ("You who are Jews . . . you who are Israelites"). His charge is that they ("the whole house of Israel," v. 36) killed Jesus through "lawless" men (a reference to the Roman executioners). Jesus was a man commended to Israel by God who worked through him for their benefit. But God's plan could not be thwarted. God reversed the shameful end of Jesus by raising him from the dead and exalting him at God's right hand. Peter makes two strong points. One is that raising Jesus from the dead, God bestowed even greater honor upon Jesus than he had in his lifetime. Two, Jesus is now a broker (signified by his place at God's right side) of God's Holy Spirit, which all have witnessed poured out on the disciples at this event. Quoting from Psalm 16:8-11 helps Peter to explain to his Israelite audience how everything that happened occurred according to God's plan. This strategy of quoting from the tradition is a plausible link to the gospel (Luke 24:13-35) in which Jesus also draws on tradition to explain why "the Messiah should suffer these things and enter into his glory" (v. 25).

### Responsorial Psalm 16:1-2, 5, 7-8, 9-10, 11

It is fitting that the psalm quoted by Peter should serve as the response to the first reading. It is basically a psalm of confidence composed by a physically sick person ("heart," "soul," "body" v. 9) whom God has rescued. At the time of this psalm's finalization, Israel did not have any notion of survival after death with God (see Psalm 6:5). But in the Hellenistic era, and after the translation of this psalm to Greek in the Septuagint (around 200 B.C.E.), there are indications that some elements in Israel began to think about immortality (of course, not the Sadducees, see Acts 23:6-8). The Hebrew verse: "I *set* the LORD ever before me" (Ps 16:8, reported in the responsorial psalm) is rendered in Greek: "I *see* the Lord before me always [that is, through all eternity]." (Ps 15:8, the Septuagint numbering of the psalms differs from the Hebrew.) This Greek version is what Luke places on the lips of Peter in his speech to "prove" that David foretold the resurrection of the body. These translation differences offer an opportunity to reflect on the historical development of faith and its understanding.

# Fourth Sunday of Easter
*Acts 2:14a, 36-41*

Scholars are generally agreed upon the idealized and idyllic account of events in the Acts of the Apostles. The number "three thousand" is historically implausible, but it dramatizes the effect of the Pentecost event and Peter's preaching. These are the first believers to be gained from among Israelites after the death of Jesus, a death for which Peter has faulted them earlier in his speech. The suspicious reader recognizes Luke's touch of restraint reflected in Peter's qualification "whomever the Lord our God will call." This acknowledges God's complete control over the growth of community of believers. The final exhortation "save yourselves from this corrupt generation" (an allusion to Deut 32:5; Ps 78:8) urges those Judeans who have accepted Jesus as Messiah to distance and separate themselves from those who have not. This separation continues to take place even at the very end of Acts (28:24-28).

## Responsorial Psalm 23:1-3a, 3b-4, 5, 6

Previously used on the Fourth Sunday of Lent (see above), this psalm is repeated today no doubt to form a bridge to the gospel (John 10:1-10) in which Jesus identifies himself as "the gate for the sheep." However, with its focus on Yahweh God as loving and caring shepherd, the psalm also links Peter's comments in the first reading about God who rescued the crucified Jesus and made him both Lord and Messiah with the gospel in which Jesus describes his function as gatekeeper of the sheepfold.

# Fifth Sunday of Easter
*Acts 6:1-7*

The Australian biblical scholar John N. Collins published a very plausible interpretation of this passage in a popularized version, *Are All Christians Ministers?* (Liturgical Press, 1992). Based on his research into relevant biblical passages including this one, his answer is a resounding "No!" The cultural context for today's reading is that the people in general spoke Greek, the apostles spoke Aramaic. Greek speaking male believers (Hellenists) complained that their widows were being excluded from the "daily ministry" (preferable to "daily distribution") by this language disparity. Greek speaking widows could not understand the Aramaic instruction given by the apostles.

In response, the Twelve are not complaining that they are being asked to set aside preaching in order to engage in menial work, "To serve at table" (NAB; NRSV) or feed the widows and thereby to "neglect the word of God." Collins proposes as a more plausible translation: "It is not right that we [Twelve] should leave aside the public proclamation of the word [in the Temple] to carry out our ministry during mealtimes of the widows."

Recall that this world is rigidly gender divided. Even families do not eat together at one table. Men eat with the boys older than puberty, and women eat separately with the girls and all the boys younger than the age of puberty. Thus the idea is not serving meals but rather carrying out this preaching activity in the vicinity of tables, i.e., at home, in private space, at gatherings of widows at tables not to eat but to learn, rather than in the public forum where Mediterranean males typically gather and discuss various topics.

The apostles come up with a solution that pleased and was accepted by the entire community. The community was to select from its midst (1) men [this is the exclusive Greek word that does not include women] of good repute (2) full of the Spirit (3) and of wisdom. In a word, the community should select men who were capable of preaching. Still, it is important to note that while the community selects them, the apostles appoint or formally commission them. Deputizing these men for the task of preaching allows the Twelve to continue to perform long prayers of praise and ministry of the Word in the Temple. Moreover, these "deacons" did not have to be with the Lord from his baptism (see Acts 1:21-22). Thus from the very beginning, the Church controlled the supply of the ministers proposed to them by the community.

Two things stand out in this passage. According to Luke, ministry involves proclaiming the Word to unbelievers (in the Temple) and nurturing the Word among believers ("at table"). Ministry, thus, is inextricably linked with purveying the Word of God, and those who do it are selected by the community and inducted into their duties by authorities in the Church.

### Responsorial Psalm 33:1-2, 4-5, 18-19

Previously used on the Second Sunday of Lent (see above) this psalm of praise celebrates the creative power of the Word (v. 4) which is an idea that was common in the sacred writings of Egypt and Babylon as it was in ancient Israel. Indeed, "word" and "works" stand in parallelism in verse 4 the divine Word is personal, effective, dependable. Further, God watches ("eye of the LORD," v. 18) over those who fear him to come to their rescue as they have need of it. The concluding verses pray that God remain faithful in extending steadfast lovingkindness (Hebrew: *ḥesed* translated by the Greek word for "mercy" as reflected in the refrain).

These verses are indeed an appropriate response to the first reading which focuses on preaching the Word of God. In addition, it bridges well to the gospel (John 14:1-12) in which Jesus clarifies his words about God's words and works in response to specific questions from Thomas and especially Philip.

# Sixth Sunday of Easter
*Acts 8:5-6, 14-17*

Today we read about the activity of Philip, one of those "deacon-ministers" selected by the community and commissioned by the apostles. He experienced incredible and instantaneous success among the Samaritans, age-old enemies of the Judeans (see 2 Kings 17; Ezra 5:1-5; etc.). The Samaritans were not only persuaded by his preaching but convinced by the signs Philip worked among them. They accepted Jesus as Messiah, and Philip baptized them. The next part of this reading often puzzles modern believers who understand that the spirit is received in baptism. In the Lukan scheme, however, the spirit is not bound to ritual or controlled by select persons. In Lukan ideology established already in the gospel and made explicit in Acts, communion with the apostles is paramount. This is what binds all the communities together. That Peter and John bestow the spirit on the Samaritans confirms their communion with the Jerusalem mother community and assures that they will remain thus united rather than form a splinter branch of believers at the very beginning of the Jesus movement. This communion with the apostles is important because they are witnesses to Jesus' resurrection (Acts 1:22), the foundational belief of the Jesus movement. This spirit is the other Advocate Jesus promised his apostles in today's gospel (John 14:15-21).

### Responsorial Psalm 66:1-3, 4-5, 6-7, 16, 20

The verses selected as a response to the first reading and bridge to the second reading praise God for the deity's "tremendous deeds" or "works." Verses 1-6 review God's mighty deeds of old, but the last part of verse 6 moves the focus to the psalmist's present: "Let us rejoice in him." This thinking typifies collectivistic personalities who even when they assume individual status (see vv. 16, 20) remain fully embedded in the collectivity. The psalmist's personal experiences are simply a prolongation of God's benevolent activity toward the chosen people.

# *The Ascension of the Lord
## Acts 1:1-11

Luke alone among the New Testament authors (here and in his gospel for this day, 24:46-53) reports Jesus' ascension as an actual visible event that took place near Bethany (Gospel) on the Mount of Olives (Acts) and was observed by "witnesses," that is, the apostles. The event takes place in an altered state of consciousness; it is a trance experience. The Greek word in v. 10 (*gazing intently* at the sky) is the word Luke uses in Acts to identify a trance experience (see e.g., Acts 7:55, etc.).

There are two kinds of trance experiences: individual and group. This is a group type of experience (recall 1 Cor 15:6 where Jesus appeared to more than five hundred at one time). According to anthropological and psychiatric studies, it is not uncommon for those who have lost loved ones in death to have vivid experiences of them for up to ten years after the event, and sometimes longer. While such experiences are especially common at the burial place, they can occur elsewhere, too.

Where do the deceased go at death? To use nontheological language, they go to alternate reality. All of reality consists of two parts: the one in which human beings presently live (called the world, ordinary reality, or culturally "normal" reality) and the one to which human beings go after they die to join God in God's realm (called alternate reality, or in theological terms "heaven," "with God," "the world to come," "the spirit world," and the like). Cultures who hold this understanding of reality know that there is an entry way between the two parts of reality: ordinary and alternate. It is a hole, or an opening, or a crack, or a door between the earth and sky which a person must find in order to go from one realm to the other. According to the sacred traditions of many cultures, that hole, or crack, or door, is located over the city in which is located the earthly abode of the deity. In Greek tradition, the hole was over Delphi. In the Israelite tradition, the hole is over Jerusalem. Thus, Jesus could not likely have ascended in Galilee (Matt 28:16), for the hole is not located there. Nor does Matthew say that. He says only that Jesus met the disciples there. Luke places the ascension at the most plausible place, where the passageway between this world and the sky is located in Israelite tradition, namely, in the environs of Jerusalem. The two men in white robes are typical of Luke and are typical representative beings from the realm of God, that is, alternate reality.

As one can expect in a trance experience, the apostles receive instruction from the risen Jesus just before he departs their company (stay in Jerusalem; wait for the Spirit; bear witness to the ends of the earth). The two messengers from the realm of God, alternate reality conclude the trance experience by promising them that Jesus will return.

### Responsorial Psalm 47:2-3, 6-7, 8-9

This enthronement psalm was sung in the Temple annually at the New Year feast when the ark of the Lord was installed anew in its place. This symbolized the Lord's definitive enthronement and was met with shouts of joy and blasts on the shofar. Non-Israelites who witnessed this event recognized the superiority of Israel's God over others. Though originating in a limited nationalistic perspective, the psalm's conclusion finds its fulfillment in the first reading and the gospel (Mark 16:15-20) for today's liturgy.

# Seventh Sunday of Easter
*Acts 1:12-14*

Mount Olivet is a significant geographical marker. The postexilic prophet Zechariah (14:1-4) said the Lord would descend here and destroy all the nations gathered against Jerusalem. In the first century c.e. a self-designated prophet from Egypt gathered a like-minded group here intending to storm Jerusalem and eject the Romans (see Acts 21:38; Josephus, *War* 2:261-163). In contrast, Jesus Messiah ascends from this location to the sky and sends the Eleven to Jerusalem on a peaceful mission, to await the Spirit. There in the Upper Room (a "high place" like Mount Olivet) the Eleven wait and devote themselves to prayer along with some women, Jesus' mother Mary, and Jesus' brothers. Luke describes the community in ideal terms, abiding in harmony and dedicating significant time to prayer, to communication with God. The perceptive reader remembers Luke's Jesus' comment that the Father will give the Holy Spirit to those who ask him (11:13). If they pray, the Spirit will come. One plausible link between this reading and the gospel (John 17:1-11a) is the final verse in which Jesus alerts the disciples that soon he will leave them "in the world" as he departs to be with the Father.

### Responsorial Psalm 27:1, 4, 7-8

The refrain (v. 7 of the psalm) reflects strong confidence that God will not abandon the psalmist as his mother and father have (v. 10, not cited today). It is a statement of unshakable faith nourished by a sense of God's presence in the Temple. In today's first reading Luke begins a motif that will permeate Acts, namely, relocation of interest from Temple to household, the new locus of God's comforting presence in the believing community. Jesus' prayer in the gospel is for his faithful followers who must remain in a hostile setting and need God's protective care. The psalm bridges both readings rather well.

# *The Vigil of Pentecost
## Genesis 11:1-9

According to the biblical account, Babylon (Babel) was the first city built by humans after the Flood. It is the first city of our era of humankind. The biblical story of Babylon further teaches that this is where humankind which had been united at that time became quite divided, and where diverse human languages originated. It was a punishment levied by God against the builders for their audacity. Extrabiblical traditions help us to fill in gaps in our high-context biblical reports. Nimrod, grandson of Ham, son of Noah, was the first "mighty man" on earth (Gen 10:8). Relying on the Greek translation (LXX), Philo of Alexandria noted that Nimrod began to be a "giant" on earth. He wanted to take revenge against God for flooding the earth and for killing his forefathers, so he decided to build a tower higher than the water could reach, perhaps even into the sky, the realm of God (see Josephus, *Antiquities* l.113-114).

The name "Babel," in Akkadian, means the "Gate of God." Thus this city, Babylon, and its tower, were intended to be the place where God and humans could meet and enter each other's territory. Since God came down to visit and look around, it seems that the technology worked (see Gen 10:8)! It is the only city in the world to which God descended to make a personal visit. But the tower which was originally intended to maintain the unity of humankind (see v. 4) begot human discord instead. The Genesis story doesn't say why, but later, extrabiblical traditions of Israel, as noted above by Josephus, do. Nimrod's plan was set in motion in contempt of God! For this, the city would eventually be destroyed.

In Israel's history, God used this city to punish Judah. Its ruler, Nebuchadnezzar, destroyed the Temple and took the elites into Exile (see Jer 20:4). But God still intended to destroy Babylon (see Isa 14:22; 21:9). After his conquest of Persia, Alexander the Great was going to make Babylon the center of his worldwide empire, but his successors abandoned the idea and the city. By the first century C.E., Babylon was in ruins and deserted, exactly the image presented by John the Revealer (Rev 17–20).

### or Exodus 19:3-8a, 16-20b

God comes to visit humans in this reading, too. God offers to make a covenant with the Israelites. If they accept—and it is always a matter of freely accepting the offer—they will be God's special possession. They must hearken to Yahweh's voice and not to the voice of any other god. The word *possession* in Hebrew and in Akkadian has the meaning of "treasures of the wealthy and of the king." This sense of the word also occurs elsewhere in the Hebrew Bible (Deut 7:6; 14:2; 26:18; Ps 135:4). Scholars are not certain of the meaning of "kingdom of priests." Since the phrase occurs with "holy nation," it can be considered somewhat synonymous. If Israel agrees to God's offer, to be special to God, it will be set apart from others (basically, that is what holy means), sacred among nations as priests are among people.

Then God appears in vv. 16-19. Like other theophanies in the Bible, this one takes place in a storm (see Exod 15:8, 10; Judg 5:4-5; Ps 18:6-19; 29; 77:16-20). The text actually mingles into the original event at Mount Sinai some elements of subsequent liturgical reenactments. For instance, the trumpet blast replicated the thunder; the furnace or fire pot replicated the smoke. This is how later generations repeated and celebrated this foundational experience with God. In the last verse, God establishes the mediating role of Moses by summoning him to the top of the mountain.

## or Ezekiel 37:1-14

"I have promised, and I will do it, says the LORD" (v. 14). What comforting words spoken by the prophet. Ezekiel reports another of his many vision experiences, an altered state of consciousness experience. Verses 2-10 report the vision while verses 11-14 (these bones are the whole house of Israel) give the explanation. Interpretation is never easy or direct because the vision is usually not linear or sequential. This means that the visionary sees many images which have to be sorted out in the interpretation. Ezekiel sees a huge number of dead, dry bones. Whose bones are these? What do they mean? Is God going to restore dead people to life? The interpretation begins in verse 11 where God identifies the bones as Israel in Babylonian Exile. God tells the prophet of the divine intent to bring these dead bones back to life, that is, to give new life to dead Israel. It is not at all a promise of restoring individual people to life.

Throughout this passage there is a play on the word "spirit" repeated in verses 1, 5, 6, 8, 9, 10, 14. The Hebrew word, *ruaḥ*, can mean the wind, breath, spirit (of God in this context). In verses 2-8, no wind, breath, or spirit is present at all. In verses 9-10, Ezekiel is commanded to pray to "the spirit," and in verse 14, God finally declares: "I will put MY spirit in you that you may live!" Altered states of consciousness experiences lend themselves to such fluidity of interpretation.

## or Joel 3:1-5

A devastating plague of locusts coupled with a drought (perhaps in the last half of the fifth century B.C.E. and the first half of the fourth century B.C.E.) are the occasion of Joel's oracle. When both these tragedies end, Joel recognizes this as a saving deed worked by Yahweh. This is a sure sign that Yahweh is present in the midst of Israel. One consequence of Yahweh's presence is a pouring out of God's spirit which produces ecstatic experience (see Num 11:24-30; 1 Sam 10:10). That old men dream dreams and young men see visions may be an indication of cultural expectations concerning altered state of consciousness experiences, but not

inflexibly. In other words, perhaps young men were enculturated to expect visions, and old men enculturated to dream.
Since both dreams and visions are among the twenty different levels of consciousness of which all human beings are
capable regardless of age, the experience can be any one of
these twenty levels. In addition to these experiences, there
are signs in the sky that Yahweh is at work rescuing Israel.

### Responsorial Psalm 104:1-2, 24, 35, 27-28, 29, 30

The refrain focuses our attention on the common element
in the four readings proposed for this vigil. "Lord, send out
your Spirit, and renew the face of the earth." In this psalm,
the poet (a very capable master of language) reflects on creation explaining why and how God the creator acts. The final
strophe is particularly appropriate. Yahweh is master of life
and death. The psalmist observes the cycle of life, death, and
new life which the Lord has established. It is evident in all of
creation, even in the life of Israel. And it is all a gift bestowed
by God's spirit.

# *Pentecost
## *Acts 2:1-11*

Luke reports yet another group type trance experience in which each member of the group becomes aware of being filled by a holy spirit. Belief in spirits was common in the ancient world, and a variety was recognized: good, malevolent, and capricious. The members here recognize that they are encountering a good or holy spirit. Luke mentions two elements of the trance: what is seen (visual) and what is heard (sound). The sound, a "noise like a strong driving wind," comes from the sky. This means it has an other-than-human source. The Israelite tradition considered thunder to be the sound of God's voice (Ps 29; Mark 1:11), though people could differ in their interpretation of the sounds they heard (John 12:29). Since the word for wind can also mean spirit, the sound indeed is of a strong wind or spirit filling the entire home. The visual element, what everyone saw in this group trance, was "tongues as of fire." This would plausibly be a red color perhaps tinged with yellow. In trance, colors identify the level of the trance, from light to deep. These colors indicate a deeper trance. The tongue shape of the fire quite likely relates to the result to which the vision plausibly contributes, namely, speaking in tongues (glossolalia). But the shape of a tongue also reminds one of a slit or opening between ordinary reality and alternate reality. If this is true, then the gathered community is at stage one of the trance (seeing geometric patterns) and Luke's report may already be anticipating what the community learned in stage two (searching for meaning in what is seen) or stage three (often arriving at totally unexpected insight).

Contemporary scholars familiar with the extensive research on glossolalia note that either Luke or his source misunderstood and therefore misinterpreted the phenomenon. In glossolalia, speech becomes musical sound. It is lexically noncommunicative, that is, this is not the informative or communicative side of discourse. Messages or insights are very rare. The musicality of glossolalia is a regular series of pulses of accented and unaccented syllables, and it is learned. One can imitate what one hears even at the first instance (see 2 Sam 10:5-12), though sometimes it occurs without a model to imitate. It is also possible that Luke deliberately speaks of foreign languages in his report (Acts 2:4, 8-11) in order to present this event as a reversal of the Babel experience of the confusion of languages (Gen 11).

Notice that the devout Judeans were divided in their assessment of the event. Some thought the speakers were drunk (see v. 13), while others believed that it was of God because they were speaking of "the mighty acts of God." As with all trance experiences, interpretation is key. In this report, the audience interprets what they hear, the speakers do not interpret what they are saying. Even in the speech he makes, Peter does not interpret what was said. He identifies the experience as an authentic trance, induced by the Spirit, and then he takes the occasion to preach about Jesus.

### Responsorial Psalm 104:1, 24, 29-30, 31, 34

Some different verses are selected from the same psalm used on the Vigil of Pentecost. Again the refrain highlights the key idea: God's spirit is an agent of renewal. It is worthwhile to ask God to send forth the Spirit to renew all creation.

# Trinity Sunday
## *Exodus 34:4b-6, 8-9*

Exodus 32–34 was inserted by an editor between two detailed descriptions of the tabernacle (Exodus 25–31, 35–39). The insert recounts the Israelites' worship of the golden calf, their severe punishment, Moses' breaking of the tablets, and the rewriting of the tablets. The purpose of this insert was to gather quite diverse traditions relative to God's self-disclosure at Sinai/Horeb. Scholars are still unable to untangle all these laws and trace them to their precise origins. Everything has been linked hindsight to Sinai/Horeb.

Today's verses focus attention on God's name in Hebrew: Yahweh (NAB: LORD). The meaning is disputed, so any interpretation one selects ought to be characterized as a personal choice. Philologically the name derives from the verb "to be" very likely in the causative form (*hiphil* "tense"). Thus one common interpretation is "I am who causes things to be," in other words, I am the creator God.

In this passage, God personally offers an interpretation of the divine nature: "merciful and gracious, slow to anger and rich in kindness and fidelity." The Hebrew for "merciful and gracious" is melodious to speak: *raḥum we ḥannun,* with the latter word only used as an attribute of God. It reminds a reader of the most important of the ninety-nine Divine Names in Islam: "Al-Rahman al Rahim," "The Compassionate, the Merciful." The Hebrew word translated "merciful" derives from the word for womb. Though some have said mercy may have been perceived as a feminine value, there is a better explanation for God describing self with this phrase.

The cultural belief is that children born from the same mother (same womb) are most closely bonded of all kin and should exhibit special concern (mercy) for one another. (See Deut 13:6 and contrast with Gen 20:12). The author of his passage presents God as positing an intimate relationship of kinship between self and God's people.

The second phrase, "kindness and fidelity," has been traditionally translated "steadfast love (Hebrew: *ḥesed*) and fidelity or loyalty *(emet)*." The phrase was used chiefly though not exclusively to describe God in the Hebrew Bible. A human being described with this phrase was a loyal, devout person. The predecessors of the Pharisees at the time of the Maccabean revolt around 167 B.C.E. were called *ḥasidim* or devout ones. Nicodemus, to whom the verses of today's gospel were addressed by Jesus (John 3:16-18), is a spiritual descendant of this group.

This is a truly remarkable insight about God's character. Though all theology is based on analogy, that is, all God-talk is rooted in human experience, these qualities contrast with what we know about Mediterranean personalities. They were quick to anger (Gen 4:1-7), unforgiving (Matt 18:23-35), and severe (Luke 9:51-56). They tended to restrict love and fidelity to real and fictive kin (Lev 19:17-18). What a shock. No wonder the sacred author presents Moses as having a keen sense of humor. His response to the meaning of God's self-disclosure might be paraphrased in this way: "Boy, do we need a God like you! We stiff-necked people are going to need your pardon many times over. If you can live with that, please join our company!"

## Responsorial Psalm: Daniel 3:52, 53, 54, 55

These verses are drawn from the hymn sung by Shadrach, Meshach, and Abednego in the furnace. The entire hymn was inserted between Daniel 3:23 and 3:24 and emphasized that heroes must be pious individuals whose wisdom is rooted in the fear of the Lord. Today's verses exhort all creatures on earth to praise God throughout the universe. The hymn was influenced by Psalm 148 which it resembles.

# Eleventh Sunday in Ordinary Time
*Exodus 19:2-6a*

God converses with Moses in an altered state of consciousness experience. The place is the mountain of God, traditionally identified as Sinai. God's message is simple: reflect on your experience of what I have done for you with regard to the Egyptians. Consider how I have cared for you. Now therefore, the choice is yours: I want you as my special possession, more precious to me than all other people. If you agree, you must obey (hearken to my voice) and keep the covenant, the sworn agreement between myself and you, my people. If you choose to live thus, you shall be a holy nation, that is, one set apart from every other nation on the earth. One plausible link of this reading to the gospel (Matt 9:36–10:8) is Jesus' charge that his disciples go only to "the lost sheep of the house of Israel," that is, to God's holy people which does not include the pagans or the Samaritans.

## Responsorial Psalm 100:1-2, 3, 5

The psalm of praise and its refrain echo well the sentiments of Exodus: "We are his people; the sheep of his flock." As the late Father Carroll Stuhlmueller points out, the Hebrew literally reports the singular "land" in verse 1, and not the plural as in our texts. He appropriately cautions against reading universal recognition and worship of Yahweh to Old Testament passages. As embarrassing as this might prove to sophisticated contemporary believers, these indeed are our inward looking ancestors in faith. They are concerned with their fellows. As noted, Matthew's Jesus shared the same restrictive view.

# Twelfth Sunday
# in Ordinary Time
*Jeremiah 20:10-13*

This passage is part of a series scattered through Jeremiah 11–20 which have been called "The Confessions of Jeremiah" or "The Intimate Papers of Jeremiah." They stem from the last period of his life from the fall of Jerusalem (597 B.C.E.) to his death in Egypt, not long after 587 B.C.E. Jeremiah's divinely inspired message was that capture by and exile in Babylon was God's will which the nation should not resist. Obviously, this is interpreted as treason. For this message Jeremiah suffered all sorts of harassment and punishment. The experience left him feeling quite isolated, abandoned, yet he felt certain this message was God's inspiration. Today's verses reflect Jeremiah's unswerving confidence in perhaps his most intense personal crisis. Former friends now have become his staunchest detractors. The confidence is rooted in God's promise to Jeremiah (1:8, 19). In all of his difficulties, Jeremiah remains fiercely loyal. Poor, in the last verse, is obviously not an economic description. It rather designates those who have temporarily lost ascribed status, reputation, honor, and who place all their hope in God to restore it. Jeremiah is supremely confident that God will vindicate him. Matthew's Jesus encourages similar confidence in today's gospel (Matt 10:26-33): "Fear no one," "do not be afraid."

## Responsorial Psalm 69:8-10, 14, 17, 33-35

Scholars point out that his psalm bears many traces of Jeremiah's influence upon the piety of Israel after his death, that is, postexilic Israel. The sentiments of the verses selected for today do indeed echo many elements of Jeremiah's prayer of confidence in the first reading. The refrain (drawn from vv. 14 and 17) captures the mood succinctly. The lowly ones, those who seek God, the poor, God's own who are in bonds, have every reason to be confident of God's help. The verses build a suitable bridge to the gospel exhortation: "do not be afraid."

# Thirteenth Sunday in Ordinary Time
## 2 Kings 4:8-11, 14-16a

Jesus' statement in today's gospel (Matt 10:37-42): "Whoever receives a prophet because he is a prophet will receive a prophet's reward." The childless woman of Shunem presses Elisha to become a regular guest. As her reward, Elisha intercedes with God to make her conceive and give birth within the year. Details help flesh out the reader's understanding. While the woman is designated literally as "a woman of substance," she does not seem to be independently wealthy. Reference to the servants of her husband (v. 22) suggest this insight. The distance from Shunem to Carmel could be traveled without stopping at Shunem. Yet the woman, who recognized Elisha as "a holy man of God," pressed him to be a guest at their home, even preparing special lodging for him.

A "holy man of God" is a type of person found in all cultures. Such a person is deemed to have access to the deity and thus is capable of brokering favors from the deity to those who seek the holy man's intercession. The holy man makes contact with the divine realm in altered states of consciousness sometimes even taking journeys to that realm (see e.g., Rev 4:1-2) to learn God's will. The narrator also attributes to Elisha great tenderness in responding to human need. Elisha's promise: "This time next year you will be fondling a baby son" contains an unusual expression (fondling or embracing) which is used to describe emotional reunions

(Gen 29:13; 33:4; 48:10) or sexual caressing (Eccl 3:5). A woman could hardly hope for a better reward.

## Responsorial Psalm 89:2-3, 16-17, 18-19

The phrase "promises of the LORD" in verse 2 refers to God's promises to David for an everlasting dynasty. Through David God would sustain good order in the world and would fulfill the covenant struck with Moses. When tragedy threatens that dynasty, the people lament and urge God to rescue them. This psalm is primarily a liturgical lament for a military defeat, but as the generalizing sentiment in the refrain indicates, the lament could relate to any experience of defeat. Moreover, the hope for rescue mirrored in these verses is rooted in God's fidelity to the divine promises. Clearly the readings (first, psalm, and gospel) are linked through the notion of "promises."

# Fourteenth Sunday in Ordinary Time
## Zechariah 9:9-10

Scholars admit the difficulty if not the impossibility of determining a specific historical context for Zechariah 9–14. It is much later than first Zechariah (about 520–518 B.C.E.). The period to which Zechariah refers is one of instability in the Judean community. People are so helpless to help themselves, God must personally come to the rescue. God stands out here as Divine Warrior. (The preferable translation is not "he shall banish" but rather "I, Yahweh, shall banish.") Judah is the bow and Ephraim the arrow (9:13-14) with which God will vanquish neighboring Pheonicia, Syria, and Philistia. God will also destroy the instruments of war (chariots, war-horses, battle bow, etc.). The king whom Yahweh will establish will be peaceable. Riding a donkey signals the peaceful intent of the rider (see Gen 49:11; 1 Kgs 1:33). The horse was an animal symbolizing pomp and used during invasion and war (see Exod 14:9; Zech 1:7-11).

Perhaps the intended link between this reading and the gospel (Matt 11:25-30) is the word "meek." God the victorious warrior-king does not "lord it over others" neither does he boast. A truly honorable Mediterranean person "understates" his position by assuming a humble posture. He takes one step behind his rightful place so that others can elevate him to his proper station. Thus even if this reading refers to an ideal human king appointed by Yahweh, the same concepts apply. This human king must be humble, mindful of his limitations, for it is indeed the Divine Warrior who saved and appointed him. This is also a good cultural context for understanding Jesus' invitation to learn of him who is meek and humble of heart.

### Responsorial Psalm 145:1-2, 8-9, 10-11, 13-14

This alphabetical psalm of praise highlights God's royal power and royal status that extend far and wide. The repetition of "king" in the refrain serves as an obvious bridge from the first reading to the gospel in which Jesus doesn't call God king but "Lord of heaven and earth," a plausible substitute for the word. Notice how Yahweh is described as "slow to anger" rather than hotheaded or hasty and abounds in steadfast love ("is gracious and merciful"). The psalmist's sentiments link the "humble" Warrior-King of Zechariah's verses with the "meek and gentle" Jesus of Matthew's verses.

# Fifteenth Sunday in Ordinary Time
## *Isaiah 55:10-11*

Chapter 55 forms the epilogue to Second Isaiah's entire work (40:1–55:13). Different parts of Isaiah 55 are read on three different Sundays in this liturgical year: the fifteenth, eighteenth, and twenty-third Sundays in Ordinary Time. Today's verses (10-11) tell of the power of God's creative word. Just as the rain-evaporation-condensation-rain cycle in nature produces new life, new growth, and new seeds, so too does God's word prove to be similarly effective. God's word is mysterious, an invisible force that still baffles contemporary believers. The word has immanent force since it springs from God's innermost recesses and reaches into the very depths of nature and humankind. Echoes of this word reverberate beyond Israel through all of creation producing beneficial effects for all of humankind. The infallible and abundant result of God's word is truly amazing. The link with today's gospel (Matt 13:1-23) is self-evident.

### Responsorial Psalm 65:10, 11, 12-13, 14

Drawn from the second half of this psalm, these verses thank God for the abundant winter rains which have made the earth bear abundant fruit. The anthropomorphic imagery of the psalm has God walking on the earth, breaking up its clods, and showering it with rain. Indeed God's chariot tracks (v. 12; see also 2 Kgs 2:1-12; Ps 69:9) now run full of water. The result is an abundant harvest.

# Sixteenth Sunday in Ordinary Time
*Wisdom 12:13, 16-19*

The literary genre of the book of Wisdom is that of rhetorical exhortation (protreptic). This is something like the formal, learned introductory lecture professors are expected to deliver when they assume a prominent appointment (chair) at a prestigious institution of higher learning. The entire book of Wisdom reflects intellectual growth and probably represents the fruits of the lifelong reflections of a very serious thinker. The author was concerned that Greek thought was exerting too strong an influence among young Israelites. Thus, writing sometime between 100 and 50 B.C.E., he sought to remind these young intellectuals of the relevance of traditional Judaic beliefs and principles which the sacred author was convinced could be compatible with Greek wisdom.

Today's verses are drawn from Part Three of this well structured book (11:15–16:1a) whose purpose is to justify God's conduct toward all human sinfulness. Specifically, today's verses reflect upon the toleration and moderation that God exhibits in the exercise of divine power. God tempers power with mercy and does not use it against the innocent. This should serve as a lesson to all to temper justice with mercy and thereby hope for mercy from God. One link with the gospel (Matt 13:24-43) is that the sower (a cipher for God) exhibits precisely the same kind of "savvy" described by the Sage in the first reading.

## Responsorial Psalm 86:5-6, 9-10, 15-16

This postexilic personal lament weaves a tissue of texts memorized from other parts of the Bible into a "new" psalm. Times of stress help one recall these memorized passages and reassure the psalmist that the Lord is indeed "good and forgiving." A verse not included in today's selection, the last stich of verse 16 helps understand the psalmist's confidence: "save the son of your handmaid." A servant born in the house of his master was deemed more faithful and dependable (see Exod 21:1ff.). His petitions stood a better chance of being heard expeditiously by the master. This psalm is a prayer well calculated to move God to pity, mercy, forgiveness.

# Seventeenth Sunday in Ordinary Time
*1 Kings 3:5, 7-12*

Solomon requested from God juridical wisdom or the ability to be a good ruler (see v. 9). Literally in Hebrew *(leb šomea)* he asked for a "hearing heart." The literal Hebrew highlights the Semitic "psychology" that permeates the Bible from beginning to end. Our ancestors in faith perceived the human person in three body zones symbolically interpreted. The zone of heart-eyes symbolized emotion-fused thinking. The zone of mouth-ears symbolized self-expressive speech. The zone of hands-feet symbolized purposeful activity. Solomon's request concerned two of these zones: hearing/understanding (mouth-ears) and heart (heart-eyes). God is pleased and blesses also the third zone in a verse not quoted today: "If you will walk in my ways, keeping my statues and my commandments, as your father David walked (notice the hands-feet vocabulary), then I will lengthen your days" (1 Kgs 3:14). Understanding must accompany and guide activity.

The link between this reading and the gospel (Matt 13:44-52) appears to be the word "understand/understanding." The relationship is superficial. The word does not have the same meaning in the original context of each reading interpreted separately. The creative preacher or interpreter will know how to handle the texts with integrity.

### Responsorial Psalm 119:57, 72, 76-77, 127-128, 129-130

In a class all by itself, this acrostic (alphabetical) psalm praises the Torah, God's law, and the joys found in observing it completely and faithfully. The 172 verses of the entire psalm utilize many synonyms for Torah: command, precepts, decrees, revelation of your words, etc. The law was never viewed as a burden but rather as God's self-disclosing speech which also revealed the divine will for those who love God. Perhaps the final verses selected for today's responsorial psalm suggested its selection as a bridge between the first reading and the gospel. The phrase "giving understanding to the simple" utilizes the same Hebrew root as the word describing what God gave to Solomon ("a listening/understanding heart").

# Eighteenth Sunday in Ordinary Time
*Isaiah 55:1-3*

In today's verses, God invites people to a banquet which provides not only food and life but personal fellowship with the deity. All human beings must eat in order to continue living. But God offers something beyond that, namely, the opportunity for establishing and confirming an intimate bond between all who share in the banquet and in divine companionship. In an earlier period of Israel's history, this bond was established between God and the Davidic king. Now, however, it will be established with all who come to Zion.

Three times in these brief verses God exhorts people to listen: "heed me," "come to me heedfully," "listen, that you may have life." There obviously is more here than simply physical nourishment. Second Isaiah plays on two meanings of the phrase "have life" thus illustrating a theme common to the Hebrew Scriptures. God gives life by providing nourishment and restores authentic meaning to life by extending to those at the table an opportunity for intimate friendship with God, if these diners will only listen. The link between this reading and the gospel (Matt 14:13-21) is clear.

## Responsorial Psalm 145:8-9, 15-16, 17-18

The verses selected from his late postexilic psalm of grateful indebtedness which was also used on the fourteenth Sunday

90

(see above) appropriately highlight the theme of divinely provided nourishment. It forms a most fitting link between the first reading and the gospel.

# Nineteenth Sunday in Ordinary Time
## 1 Kings 19:9a, 11-13a

Yet again have the architects of the Lectionary created a new Scripture by carving today's verses from their fuller context. This version of Elijah's encounter with God in an altered state of consciousness does not mention his discouragement and despair even to the point of asking God to let him die (1 Kgs 19:3-4)! Instead, Elijah appears in these edited verses as a person of trust with whom God communicates intimately. Neither is God's word of rebuke to Elijah (v. 13b) included in today's reading.

The sacred author records traces of Exodus in this passage which encourage the reader to compare Elijah with Moses. "Horeb" is the name that the Elohist and Deuteronomist give to the mountain of God which the Yahwist and the Priest traditions call "Sinai." Mention of this mountain is likely the intended link with today's gospel (Matt 14:22-33) where Jesus goes up to a mountain to pray. The cave is more plausibly a shallow cleft in the rock of the kind that pockmark the Judean hills and provides shade and shelter to humans and animals alike. This allusion is intended to stir memory of "the hollow of the rock" where God tells Moses to rest while God's glory "passes by." Just as Moses was the mediator who brokered the covenant between Yahweh (Israel's Patron) and Israel (Yahweh's client), so is Elijah to reestablish the covenant and restore Israel to its pristine faith.

Scholars note that the Elijah-Elisha stories illustrate how prophets, specialists in God's will for their contemporary times, met the basic life-needs of common folk who suffered under government abuse and famine. Elijah's discouragement probably reflects the growing doubt among a segment of northern Israel that the Omri dynasty (880 B.C.E. to 873 B.C.E.) could save them. Only faith in Yahweh would do.

### Responsorial Psalm 85:9, 10, 11-12, 13-14

These verses reflect Canaanite mythology. They annually celebrated Baal's conquest of winter and its hostile forces that churned up the Mediterranean. His victory resulted in a quiet spring time allowing new life to emerge from the soil and the flocks. The verses are located within a very long national lament and prayer asking God to restore the intimate covenant bond with Israel. As winter could upset the order of creation, so too could infidelity to the covenant cause God to work havoc in creation. Those who fear God and act justly can expect God to restore order to creation.

# Twentieth Sunday in Ordinary Time
## Isaiah 56:1, 6-7

This chapter begins the last ten chapters of Isaiah known since 1892 as Third (or Trito-) Isaiah. This author was familiar with the eighth century Isaiah, as well as Second Isaiah, the great prophet of the sixth-century Exile. Third Isaiah preached a simple message around 520 B.C.E., the same time during which the prophets Haggai and Zechariah were active. The opening verse contrasts two word pairs: right and just; salvation and justice. The first forms part of an imperative: this is what the returned exiles must adopt as their lifestyle. If they do, God will establish salvation and justice.

Who will constitute this revivified community? Those who previously were excluded: eunuchs and foreigners (see Deut 23:2-8). These foreigners however must exhibit firm commitment to Yahweh. They must join themselves to the Lord, minister to him, love the Lord, and serve him. They must keep the Sabbath and observe the covenant. If they do, Yahweh personally will bring them to Zion and make them rejoice in the Temple, for that house of prayer shall be called "a house of prayer for all peoples." Today's gospel (Matt 15:21-28) in which a non-Israelite woman struggles to win a favor from Jesus suggests that Third-Isaiah's oracle might not have sunk into his listeners' minds nor into the community's convictions.

### Responsorial Psalm 67:2-3, 5, 6, 8

This is a psalm of grateful indebtedness expressed to God for a bountiful harvest. Mention of that harvest in verse 8, however, has been curiously omitted from today's verses. Thus the sentiments of gratitude are generic. It is no doubt because of the references to the nations (v. 5) and peoples (v. 6) that these verses have been paired with the first reading to serve also as a bridge to the gospel. The high number of parallels between the Hebrew vocabulary of this psalm and Ugaritic (a Northwest Semitic language) creates a suspicion that it may have originally be a non-Israelite composition. The priestly prayer of Numbers 6:24-26 reflected in verse 1 probably served to gain it acceptance. The universal features of the psalm (all the peoples; all the nations) might also have been added under the influence of Second and Third Isaiah.

# Twenty-First Sunday in Ordinary Time
*Isaiah 22:19-23*

Shebna and Eliakim were stewards (like chancellors) in the royal household, the former condemned and rejected, the latter endorsed and commended (see 2 Kgs 18:18; Isa 36:3 and 37:2). The actual historical sequence is that Eliakim held the office but was succeeded by Shebna. When Shebna failed, Eliakim was restored. What Isaiah reports in these verses is not history but a promissory oracle. The description of Elkiah as the good steward to succeed Shebna is cast in the language of royal, Davidic ideology. Isaiah is describing a forthcoming ideal steward who will be similar to the expected ideal good king-messiah. As the king-messiah will be "father forever" (Isa 9:5), so the ideal steward will be "father to the inhabitants of Jerusalem" (v. 21). As the royal messiah will have a house and kingdom that will endure forever (2 Sam 7:16), the coming steward will be "in a sure spot" (the key Hebrew word is *'amen* = forever; sure). This ideal steward will have full control and regulate access to the king ("key" v. 22). He will be a "peg," the center of administrative power upon whom everything in the royal household will depend. Such a person will ensure a pure, perfect, and secure royal administration.

One possible association with today's gospel (Matt 16:13-20) is as background for Peter's identification of Jesus as Messiah.

## Responsorial Psalm 138:1-2, 2-3, 6, 8

To interpret this psalm with appropriate sensitivity, it is important to review two Mediterranean cultural concepts: collectivistic personality and the impropriety of saying thank you. This psalm like others has been identified as an "individual psalm of thanksgiving." However, to say "thank you" in the Middle East is to terminate a relationship (see Luke 17:16), a very foolish cultural decision since one never knows when one might need this person's favor again, unless as in the case of the Samaritan "leper" one is not likely to encounter that Judean benefactor again. Thus Claus Westermann correctly suggested that these "thanksgiving psalms" be more appropriately named "narrative praise of the individual." In cultures whose core value is honor, the appropriate response to favors, to grace, to gifts is to sing the praises of the benefactor. What the beneficiary expressed to the benefactor is indebtedness, a sense of obligation which can never be completely repaid. The English statement would be "Much obliged," or "I owe you," or "I owe you big time!" or something in that vein.

Yet Westermann errs in identifying these sentiments as coming from an "individual." It is more correct to understand and interpret the "I" in this and other similar psalms as a collectivistic individual. Such a person hardly ever discloses his name but is content to be identified by the patriarch or the family. Such a person does not want to stand out from the crowd but is instead only too happy to disappear into it. Thus, in this psalm dominated by "I," the final verse (and today's refrain) asks God not to forsake "the work of your hands." Though an individualist would probably think of God's creation of the first earthling (Gen 2:7) or the psalmist's expression of praise for his own conception (Ps 139, esp. vv. 13-15), those Mediterranean persons who heard that phrase ("the work of your hands") would think of the collectivity "Israel" as described by Isaiah (60:21; 64:7).

As an expression of grateful indebtedness, these psalm verses serve as a good link between the first reading in which Eliakim benefits from God's free choice and the gospel in which Peter, too, ought to attribute his insight to Jesus' heavenly Father.

# Twenty-Second Sunday in Ordinary Time
*Jeremiah 20:7-9*

The time is the summer of 594 B.C.E. The Judeans are in Babylonian Exile. An unsuccessful coup in January of that year against Nebuchadnezzar stirred hopes among the exiles that perhaps the next attempt will succeed. Deposed King Zedekiah summons ambassadors from Edom, Moab, Ammon, Tyre, and Sidon hoping to form a coalition that can get rid of Nebuchadnezzar. The prophet Hananiah announces an end to the Exile within two years. Jeremiah's prophecy, however, is that things will only get worse before they get better. Tired of hearing his incessant message of gloom and doom, Jeremiah's enemies make life miserable for him. It is out of this misery that today's verses spring. His message used to fill Jeremiah with joy and happiness (15:16). Now they occasion derision and reproach (20:8).

The Hebrew words Jeremiah uses to describe how God affected him are most often used in the context of sexual seduction (duped—Exod 22:15; and too strong for me = seized or overpowered me—Prov 7:13). God enticed Jeremiah to be a spokesperson, but Jeremiah's experience of this role has been embittering since nothing but hardship and suffering has been his lot. One way to put an end to this experience is to stop communicating. Easier said than done. The word of Yahweh reflects the deity's very nature which the Bible describes as a "consuming fire" (Exod 24:17). Jeremiah cannot

hold it in; he must preach it and bear the personal consequences which are no less painful than trying to keep the
words in his heart and not preach them. The link with
today's gospel (Matt 16:21-27) is Jesus' compulsion to speak
God's will for him painful as it was for himself and for others
to hear it.

### Responsorial Psalm 63:2, 3-4, 5-6, 8-9

The sentiments of these psalm verses form a good bridge
between the first reading and the gospel. The thirst for God is
a yearning to return to intimacy which once experienced does
indeed leave one wishing for more. It was thus with Jeremiah
and certainly with Jesus. Each experienced God quite intimately and personally (the word "gaze" refers to a special
level of consciousness in which God most often communicates with creatures; it leaves the creature breathless). That
experience "is a greater good than life." Coming close to the
ark, the psalmist feels embraced by the wings of the cherubim
which remind him once more of the intimate embrace of a
loving God.

# Twenty-Third Sunday in Ordinary Time
*Ezekiel 33:7-9*

These verses resume the theme of watchman which was introduced earlier (Ezek 3:16-21). During the day, some residents of walled cities worked in the fields outside the wall. The watchman was to keep a keen eye on the horizon. If an enemy approached, he would warn the citizens and urge them to return to safety within the walls. People ignored that warning at their own peril. Ezekiel was to warn the wicked to repent. If he failed to perform his mission diligently, the sinner would get his just desserts, but Ezekiel would be held accountable for his perdition. If the wicked ignore Ezekiel's exhortations, their fate is their own fault. God desires the repentance of sinners, not their death. This reading is clearly related to the gospel (Matt 18:15-20) in which Jesus offers a strategy for calling an erring member of the believing community back to his or her senses or suffer the consequences.

### Responsorial Psalm 95:1-2, 6-7, 8-9

"If today you hear his voice," whether it be God's, Ezekiel's, Jesus' or a fellow believer's, the advice is to pay attention. The verses selected for today are drawn chiefly from the sections in which God is praised. Yet lest the pilgrims to the Jerusalem Temple lose themselves reveling in memories of God's goodness, the psalmist reminds them that it is as easy now as it was in the past to test God, to forget God. They should remain attentive and obedient.

# Twenty-Fourth Sunday in Ordinary Time
### Sirach 27:30–28:7

It is a good idea to remember that "sin" in ancient Middle Eastern culture is best understood as shaming another, whether that be God or a fellow human being. Shame is no light matter in this culture; it always requires revenge. Read in this context, Sirach's reflections can be better understood. He is not anticipating Christian views, because even today's gospel (Matt 18:21-35) may be more about forgoing revenge than forgiveness in its sophisticated contemporary theological understanding. Since the most important thing in this culture is honor, a person with a right to take revenge who would forgo that right gains even more honor than he would by exacting his rightful pound of flesh.

Moreover, Sirach reminds his readers of God's right to revenge when the deity is shamed. If God were to exact what was due, what human being could stand it? (see Lev 26:1-26). Thus if a "sinful" human being with a right to revenge were to forgo that right, he would be in a position to "shame" (in the sense of "force") God to acting even more honorably toward himself the sinner by forgoing divine revenge as did the sinner toward a fellow ethnic. The concluding exhortations to "remember" the end (last days, death and decay) and the commandments could well be a reminder of God's call to "love your neighbor as yourself" (Lev 19:17) and "overlook faults" (Sir 28:7).

**Responsorial Psalm 103:1-2, 3-4, 9-10, 11-12**

Those who fear the Lord, that is, those who remember who the Lord is and who they are, will experience the Lord's surpassing steadfast loving kindness *(ḥesed)*. God will pardon, heal, redeem, and treat sinners with kindness and compassion. We are blessed indeed that God does not deal with us according to our sins or crimes.

# Twenty-Fifth Sunday in Ordinary Time
## *Isaiah 55:6-9*

These final thoughts of Second (exilic) Isaiah are addressed to the scoundrel and the wicked who perhaps ought not be too hastily identified as "sinners." Old Testament scholar Walter Brueggemann suggests that these may be people who are considering or perhaps even have already decided to ignore God's call through Isaiah to return from Babylon to Jerusalem. Maybe they have grown comfortable in Babylon and are reluctant to give that up. Or maybe they find God's promise of renewal too difficult to believe. These may be the thoughts and ways that are not God's thoughts and ways. At the very least, this interpretation would seem to meet the requirement of a proper understanding of Second Isaiah in his historical and cultural context. Clearly the link between this reading and today's gospel (Matt 20:1-16a) is intended to be made on a different level. In Jesus' parable about God (the owner of the vineyard), God chooses to behave like a gracious Mediterranean Patron (God's ways) but can behave like an account keeping employer (human ways) if creatures prefer to think they can hold God to a contract.

### Responsorial Psalm 145:2-3, 8-9, 17-18

This acrostic (alphabetic) psalm is principally a psalm of praise. Today's verses clearly manifest that both directly (vv. 2-3) and indirectly (vv. 8-9, 17-18) by mentioning God's nature and deeds deserving of praise.

# Twenty-Sixth Sunday in Ordinary Time
*Ezekiel 18:25-28*

The context for these verses is actually set at the beginning of this chapter: "Fathers have eaten green grapes, thus their children's teeth are on edge" (Ezek 18:2). It was a longstanding belief in Israel that children of parents who were sinners would inherit their punishment, while children of righteous parents would inherit their blessings. Ezekiel countered this by preaching about individual responsibility. His preaching however was met with resistance from the offspring of righteous parents: "The LORD'S way is not fair!!! I deserve the blessings of my righteous parents no matter what kind of person I might be, and the children of sinners rightly deserve their sorry lot." In typical Mediterranean fashion, Ezekiel responds sarcastically: "Thus says the LORD: . . . are not YOUR ways unfair?" If a righteous person fails, or a sinner repents, each should receive an appropriate personal judgment. The link intended between this reading and today's gospel (Matt 21:28-32) is located in Jesus' question: "Which one [of two sons] did his father's will?" and then his application of the insight to the audience.

### Responsorial Psalm 25:4-5, 6-7, 8-9

In this acrostic (alphabetic) psalm, an individual sinner, mindful of his shortcomings, asks God for guidance, compassion, and indulgence. He concludes with a confident assertion that God will not ignore the humble, those who know their proper place in relationship to God.

# Twenty-Seventh Sunday in Ordinary Time
*Isaiah 5:1-7*

This segment of Isaiah's message dates from the early years of his ministry (783–742 B.C.E.). It is a carefully and cleverly constructed parable. The Hebrew word translated "friend" can also be rendered "beloved," so the listener at first expects to hear a heart-warming love ballad. Alas for all the loving care he lavished on his vineyard (a word used to describe the beloved in the Canticle), it brought forth rotten, stinking grapes. Something went wrong in the love affair. If this parable refers to the relationship of Yahweh and his people, the rotten grapes are the fruit of infidelity, namely, illegitimacy.

Verses 3-5 invite the listeners to render judgment on the Lord God's decision to publicly denounce the infidelity. Lest anyone miss the point, verse 7 specifies that the unfaithful partner is the house of Israel, the people of Judah. The infidelity is radical. In a masterful play on Hebrew words, a strategy by which a man demonstrates his manliness and his mastery of language and tradition, Isaiah lays out God's case. God looked for judgment (*mišpat*, the fulfillment of God's total will for humankind), but found instead bloodshed *(mispah)*. God searched for justice (*ṣedaqa*, any aspect of living out God's total will), but found instead an outcry sparked by injustices *(ṣeʾaqa)*. The link to the gospel (Matt 21:33-43) is the common reference to vineyard, though in Isaiah the problem is the vineyard, that is, Israel itself, while in Matthew the problem is with the tenant farmers, the leadership of Israel.

**Responsorial Psalm 80:9, 12, 13-14, 15-16, 19-20**

This national lament utilizes the vine imagery to review the history of Israel's experience but also to move God to compassion. The vine God transplanted from Egypt grew from the Mediterranean to the Euphrates. Yet God allowed Assyria and other nations to lay it waste. The psalmist asks God to restore the beloved nation with a promise that it will never again abandon God.

# Twenty-Eighth Sunday in Ordinary Time
*Isaiah 25:6-10a*

Today's verses are drawn from a section of Isaiah (24–27) dubbed the "little apocalypse" or "The Apocalypse of Isaiah." Most likely it originated in the late sixth or early fifth century B.C.E. One feature of this literary form (apocalypse) is that the author seems to have lost all hope and confidence in human effort in the political-historical realm. The frustrating experience of futility with human efforts caused these authors to leave everything directly in God's hands. As the described events unfold, human beings become patient and fascinated though they are nothing more than totally inactive bystanders. These chapters from Isaiah reflect such an outlook, though the prophet has not entirely broken all links with worldly realities. Observe the three references to "this mountain" (vv. 6, 7, 10a) referring to Mount Zion.

In these verses, Isaiah describes what is called an eschatological banquet which is a symbol for eternal happiness. God personally caters this banquet and features the best that is available to eat and drink. However, the heart of Isaiah's good news is that God will destroy death understood not as in the West, as a punctiliar event. Rather, God will destroy death as a negative force that diminishes life at every level in every way. Actually, Isaiah gives his message a splendid Mediterranean cultural ring: God will remove the reproach, that is the shame of his people. In the Mediterranean world, loss of honor is tantamount to death. Restoration of honor brings joy, fulfillment, peace, and every imaginable good thing. God has done what no one else could.

The link to the gospel (Matt 22:1-14) is obviously the theme of a banquet, a feast. But the readings offer a contrast. Isaiah depicts a people who accept the feast and are grateful. Jesus describes a people who reject the invitation, and even among those who accept one acts totally out of cultural character. It's equivalent to shooting oneself in the foot.

### Responsorial Psalm 23:1-3a, 3b-4, 5, 6

This most popular of all the psalms forms a very fitting bridge between the first reading and the gospel. It hymns the gracious and benevolent God who leads the people on their way, both as a nation and as individual collectivistic persons. This God also sustains the people with the necessities of life in the very face of those who would destroy them. That sense very likely overpowers the image of good nourishment. Indeed, the confidence of being able to reside securely at peace in this land and frequent the Temple on pilgrimage, there to celebrate with God, prompts a deep sense of grateful indebtedness.

# Twenty-Ninth Sunday in Ordinary Time
## *Isaiah 45:1, 4-6*

Second Isaiah, the author of chapters 40–55 in the book by his name makes quite a contrast to the first thirty-nine chapters. The intended recipients of these declarations are no longer in Jerusalem but rather now in Babylon, in exile. This prophet does not condemn nor threaten. He rather gives consolation and hope. A plausible date for these particular chapters is the latter part of the Exile, toward 537 B.C.E.

These verses are cast in a form known as a "royal decree." The form serves to present God as addressing a king in order to instruct him, or perhaps to bestow power, legitimacy, or authorization upon him. God does a shocking thing here. God names Cyrus, the Persian, a pagan, as God's very own anointed, a Messiah! The title was never used for the Promised One of the messianic age in the Scriptures but was rather used mainly for kings (see 1 Sam 16:6), and occasionally for prophets (Ps 105:15) and priests (Lev 4:3). This non-Israelite Cyrus is chosen by God to carry out the divine will to save. Yet, even Cyrus did not know this (v. 4)! Perhaps that is Isaiah's great insight here. God can and does use the most unlikely of human agents to carry out the divine will. So often, God's will is brought to fulfillment in ways believers neither expect nor prefer.

The link between this reading and today's gospel (Matt 22:15-21) is rather superficial, namely two political rulers:

Cyrus and Caesar. Yet it reminds us that in the ancient Mediterranean world there was no "separation of Church and state," a situation that still exists in parts of that world today. Countries were theocracies, and the shameful experience of Israel in Isaiah's and Jesus' time is that a ruler other than Yahweh was actually in charge.

### Responsorial Psalm 96:1, 3, 4-5, 7-8, 9-10

There could be no more fitting response to the first reading than this enthronement psalm honoring Yahweh as king of Israel. The refrain based on verse 7 ("Give the Lord glory and honor") is actually borrowed Psalm 29:1, with an ideological correction: "families of nations" replaces "you sons of God." The psalmist also borrowed from Second Isaiah (40:10; 44:23; 49:13). He invites Israel to praise God-king (vv. 1-3) and offers a reason why it should (vv. 4-6). Then he invites all nations to join in this praise (vv. 7-9) and once again offers a good reason (v. 10).

# Thirtieth Sunday in Ordinary Time
*Exodus 22:20-26*

Exodus 20:22–23:19 is the oldest collection of laws in the Hebrew Bible. It is known as the Book of the Covenant (see Exodus 24:7). The contents of this book quite likely originated as individual laws which were gathered into subcollections already in the premonarchic period. This law code was obviously an expression of God's will but not comprehensively so. This means that the law code gives a sample of the divine will for Israel and appoints Moses (and his successors) as the mediator.

Why are the resident alien, widow, and orphan singled out for special attention? Because they are "poor," which is not primarily an economic designation. It rather designates a temporary loss of status, one's honorable standing in a community. (See the debate in the Pastorals [1 Tim 5:3-16] concerning who are "truly widows.") The alien is living apart from his community of origin, a widow has lost her husband, and an orphan has lost a parent. None of these statuses is viewed as permanent. Indeed the person in question is expected to take action to regain the lost status. The alien can return to his people of origin, the widow can either remarry or return to the care of her father or brother, and so too can the orphan move to other kin. The prohibition against molesting or oppressing or wronging these people is a prohibition against thwarting their efforts to regain lost status.

Notice that in each case, there is a reminder: Israelites once were aliens in Egypt; they can also become widows and orphans in their own setting. Hence in brief, Israel should treat others as they would want to be treated in an identical situation.

The law about lending money or taking a cloak as a security deposit is best understood in the context of the pervasive cultural belief that all goods are limited. There are no more where these came from. To demand interest is to expect the person to somehow come up with more than he was given to temporarily replace what he had. Where would he get it? It didn't exist! (It was perfectly permissible, however, to take interest from foreigners.) So too with the cloak as security deposit. Where would he get another?

The ideological underpinning for these laws is that if one behaves unkindly toward fellow Israelites, God will behave in like manner toward the guilty Israelite. Among Israelites, God will personally intervene if one should deprive another of a necessity. The link between this reading and today's gospel (Matt 22:34-40) is that it offers concrete illustrations of what it means to love God above all and "love your neighbor as yourself."

### Responsorial Psalm 18:2-3, 3-4, 47, 51

This is a king's song of thanksgiving for rescue from a difficult situation. The verses selected for today's liturgy only report the beginning and end of the psalm, so they do not treat of the situation from which the king found rescue. The sentiments carved from the psalm, however, fit the reading. God is responsible for the king's rescue, and the king piles up divine attributes to underscore that: my strength, my rock, my fortress, my deliverer, my shield, the horn of my salvation, my stronghold, my savior. There is no mistaking who is really responsible for the king's well-being.

# Thirty-First Sunday in Ordinary Time
*Malachi 1:14b–2:2b, 8-10*

Regrettably, the key to understanding these verses from Malachi have not been included in today's reading. "A son honors his father, and a servant his master. If then I am father, where is my honor? And if I am master, where is my fear?" (Mal 1:6). God deserves honor and should be respected, yet the priests have done neither. They have "despised" (= shamed) God (v. 6). How? They did not "lay it to heart," (Mal 2:2), that is, they did not take God nor their obligations as priest to God seriously. Their obligation was to give torah, instruction, but they deviated from this and instead "caused many to falter" by their instruction (Mal 2:8). Instead of conserving the truth of God's instruction, they despised it. For this reason, God will make them despicable before all the people whom they were to serve with reliable instruction. They will be cursed by God. The notion that links this reading with the gospel (Matt 23:1-12) is the responsibility of leaders to their followers. The Pharisees teach correctly but do not practice what they preach. The priests criticized by Malachi do not even teach correctly. Leaders ought not to inflate their honor or reputation to the detriment of those who depend upon them. Religious authorities should empower rather than disenfranchise their subjects.

### Responsorial Psalm 131:1, 2, 3

It is difficult to appreciate this psalm as a response to the reading from Malachi. One can read the sentiments smugly:

"I'm not like THEM!" It is possible also to read it from an anti-intellectual perspective: "I'm simple like an infant. I don't bother myself about 'things too sublime for me.'" Perhaps this brief psalm is best interpreted from the perspective of verse 3: "Hope in the LORD, both now and forever." Hope in Middle Eastern culture is trust, placing all one's eggs, so to speak, in the other's basket. Thus, to avoid being disappointed in or betrayed by human authorities who presumably speak God's will, it is wise to rely solely and exclusively on God. In this one finds peace.

# Thirty-Second Sunday in Ordinary Time
## *Wisdom 6:12-16*

Written in Alexandria between 100 and 50 B.C.E., the book of Wisdom strives to assure Judeans that their ancient traditions are in no way inferior to Hellenism which has been growing more and more appealing since Alexander conquered the world and spread Greek wisdom. Today's verses are drawn from that section of this well-crafted literary masterpiece which describe Solomon's search for Wisdom. The sacred author proposes the quest of Solomon as a model deserving imitation. Specifically these verses report the easy accessibility of wisdom. She is presented as an appealing woman who searches for her admirers whom she will bless and lead to a life of holiness. (Wisdom ultimately, of course, is God or one of God's functions.) The original audience of these reflections recognized clear allusions to the Egyptian deity, Isis, goddess of culture and benefactor of humanity. She was worshiped throughout the Aegean world. Yahweh sends his throne partner, Lady Wisdom (looking very much like Isis) to minister to the chosen people. Thus it is Yahweh and not any one in Hellenistic culture that is the true benefactor of Israel. The link with today's gospel (Matt 25:1-13) is quite likely the mention of five wise wedding attendants.

### Responsorial Psalm 63:2, 3-4, 5-6, 7-8

What could be "a greater good than life"? (v. 4). Only God! No wonder the psalmist thirsts and pines for God, seeks God with determination and diligence. The context of the psalm may have been some sorrowful situation in which God seemed remote, even absent. But the psalmist sings with confidence. God does not abandon the creatures who are precious objects of divine love. The psalmist meditates on the fidelity of God, remembers previous rescues, and is certain God will satisfy his every desire beyond expectation.

# Thirty-Third Sunday in Ordinary Time
*Proverbs 31:10-13, 19-20, 30-31*

Following many scholars, it is possible to interpret this passage as an allegorical description of personified Wisdom. As the "fear of the Lord is the beginning of knowledge" (Prov 1:7), so "the woman who fears the LORD is to be praised" (Prov 31:30). Thus the final poem forms an inclusion with the statement of the book's motif at the beginning. From this perspective it is possible to link this paean to the ideal wife with the praise of the faithful, vigilant, responsible, and honest third servant of today's gospel (Matt 25:14-30).

Yet even an allegory needs some root in reality, else it wouldn't be understood. The reality here is an ideal wife, and the emphasis ought to be on ideal. In the Middle Eastern world, the ideal is treasured more than the reality. The reality in these verses is more likely an elite woman rather than a peasant. Yet this person serves as an ideal worthy of imitation. What rings true to reality is that in Middle Eastern culture, women indeed are the ones expected to engage in planned and calculated activities such as are described in these select verses. Men, in contrast, are given more to spontaneous responses to the inspiration of the moment. If a friend invites one for coffee, one accepts the invitation even if one were on the way to performing a task, even a necessary task. The Italians would say "domani" (Tomorrow!). Today is for enjoying the opportunity of the moment. From this "real" perspective, the third servant in the gospel is like the ideal wife in that knowing his master was greedy, he nevertheless calculated the cost to him and did the honest thing with the entrusted money. He preserved it and didn't risk losing it.

### Responsorial Psalm 128:1-2, 3, 4-5

It is interesting to pray this psalm about the righteous man who fears the LORD in response to a reading extolling a righteous woman who fears the LORD. It is quite likely an unintended humorous pairing "corrected" by the refrain. The psalm originally might have been sung to send the Jerusalem-pilgrim on the homeward journey. The psalmist blesses the pilgrim and pronounces the joy that will be realized in work and family. Fearing the LORD will always prompt a believer to choose the right course of action no matter what the consequences.

# Thirty-Fourth Sunday in Ordinary Time (Christ the King)
*Ezekiel 34:11-12, 15-17*

Ezekiel addresses these present words of salvation to the exiles after the fall of Jerusalem (587 B.C.E.). In these verses, Ezekiel presents the "good news" that follows the "bad news" he just described, namely, that the human rulers of Israel had failed miserably. Now God personally will look after the sheep. Applying the image of a shepherd to rulers was a favorite and widespread practice in the ancient Near East from Sumerian (fourth millennium B.C.E.) to Neo-Babylonian times. In the Bible, it was especially popular with Jeremiah (2:8; 3:15; 10:21; 22:22; 23:1-4; 25:34-37; 50:6). But verse 17 which actually begins the next section (vv. 17-22) shifts attention away from the shepherd to the sheep themselves. God will judge between "one sheep and another, between rams and goats" (v. 17). The rams and male goats symbolize the strong, the elite, the wealthy who preyed upon the weaker sheep, namely, the poor. The wealthy hoarded the "pastures" for themselves and deprived the poor of access to subsistence. The divisions of Judah's stratified society thus made it an easy target for Nebuchadnezzar. God will reverse that by disempowering the strong and giving the weak a better chance to survive, indeed to thrive. The obvious if superficial link with today's gospel (Matt 25:31-46) is quite likely verse 7 with its reference to sheep, rams, and he-goats.

**Responsorial Psalm 23:1-2, 2-3, 5-6**

This most popular of psalms in the Psalter is an obviously fitting choice as a response to the reading from Ezekiel. The LORD is indeed the best shepherd a sheep could wish for. In him, the sheep—the hungry, thirsty, stranger, naked, ill, and others in today's gospel—find their actual redeemer when fellow human beings fail, or worse yet aggravate the problem.

# Recommended Resources

## Old Testament

Craghan, John F. *Psalms for All Seasons*. Collegeville, Minn.: The Liturgical Press, 1993.

Gottwald, Norman K. *The Hebrew Bible: A Socio-Literary Introduction*. Minneapolis, Minn.: Fortress Press, 1985.

Holladay, William L. *Long Ago God Spoke: How Christians May Hear the Old Testament Today*. Minneapolis, Minn.: Fortress Press, 1995.

Stuhlmueller, Carroll, C.P. *Psalms*. 2 vols. Old Testament Message. Wilmington, Del.: Michael Glazier, 1983.

_____. *The Spirituality of the Psalms*. Collegeville, Minn.: The Liturgical Press, 2002.

## Cultural World of the Bible

Pilch, John J. *The Cultural World of Jesus, Sunday by Sunday: Cycle A*. Collegeville, Minn.: The Liturgical Press, 1995.

_____. *The Cultural Dictionary of the Bible*. Collegeville, Minn.: The Liturgical Press, 1999.

_____. *The Triduum: Breaking Open the Scriptures*. Collegeville, Minn.: The Liturgical Press, 2000.

_____. *The Cultural World of the Apostles. The Second Reading, Sunday by Sunday, Year A*. Collegeville, Minn.: The Liturgical Press, 2001.

Pilch, John J. and Bruce J. Malina, eds. *Handbook of Biblical Social Values*. Peabody, Mass.: Hendrickson Publishers, 1998.

## Websites

Roman Catholic Lectionary for Mass
http://clawww.lmu.edu/faculty/fjust/Lectionary.htm

Revised Common Lectionary
http://divinity.library.vanderbilt.edu/lectionary

*Cultural World of Jesus* (Pilch)
http://www.liturgy.slu.edu